Write from Your Heart

Discover Your Author Voice Through Journaling

No one is more qualified to write about your life than you

Wendy Fry

Today, tomorrow, every day of your life write from your heart

Whether you're an aspiring or published author Wendy Fry - Writing Coach, Ghostwriter and Therapist with over twenty years in the writing and wellbeing industry will empower you to set and achieve your writing goals. Offering transformational, simple, and practical strategies, you will discover your innate confidence and creativity to attract the success you deserve.

www.wendyfry.com

General Information

Legal Information

Disclaimer: The ideas in Write from Your Heart represent those of the author as of the date of publication. The book is for informational and educational purposes only to aid and support emotional wellbeing and personal development.

The information in this book is not a substitute for professional medical advice.

If you are suffering from any physical or psychiatric condition, please seek the help of the appropriately qualified health professional. Any use of information in this book is at the reader's discretion and risk.

The author and publisher cannot be held responsible for any loss, claim, or damage arising out of use, or misuse, of the suggestions made, or the failure to take medical advice.

ISBN Number: 978-1-9163531-0-7

Publisher: Wendy Fry Publishing

Orders: Signed copies of Write from Your Heart with a personalised dedication and bulk discounts are available. You can contact the author at www.wendyfry.com

Paperback and e-book via www.amazon.co.uk and www.amazon.com

Call to Action

Wendy welcomes your support.

- ✓ Leave a review on Amazon
- ✓ Gift a copy of the book to your loved ones
- ✓ Join the 'Random Acts of Kindness' movement gifting a copy of the book in a random place
- ✓ Share details of Wendy's website and services www.wendyfry.com

Thank you for your love, kindness and support. Your willingness to share this book lights the way for others to see their way out of the dark.

Much love,

Wendy x

Journaling Disclaimer

Journaling has many benefits and may help overcome a range of emotional and mental health issues though it cannot take the place of medical or mental health support. Please do contact a healthcare professional for the relevant guidance based on your specific needs.

This book is not a substitute for the medical advice of physicians or mental health practitioners.

You are welcome to contact the author to enquire about support programmes, workshops and training courses at www.wendyfry.com on the understanding her services relate to emotional health & wellbeing, writing coaching and mentoring only.

Reader Dedication

I am writing this book for you. I see beneath the mask you wear and the façade you think you must play out. I see the beauty deep within your soul.

I write from my heart to yours to acknowledge you. Look how far you've come. Take a bow and celebrate your life lived thus far.

I am possibly no different from you. I know what it's like to hurt and to play small. I feel what you feel, and I know you want to heal. I know you have a gift to share. The gift of your experience. Your story and the voice of your heart matters. We both know if you do not begin to write now, your story stays untold.

I don't know how you came across 'Write from Your Heart' or how it found you. I trust, when we are ready to accept an invitation and fulfil our calling the right person, book or experience turns up at the right time.

Dare to be all of who you are. Tell your story. Write from your heart and your words will not fail you.

What's the best that can happen when you do?

Supporting you on your author's journey. Now, is the time to write from your heart!

Benefits of Using Write from Your Heart Methodology – Here's what others are saying:

''There is a possibility that I could fall in love with writing. Your work and teachings are so powerful.'' Louise.

''All I can say is "WOW" what an inspiring person you are. Sometimes the little tips and those amazing MASSIVE shifts can be so valuable.'' Ann.

''I realise those books I've started with more dedication will get middles and the ones in mid-stage will get endings when I put my heart and mind to it! Cheers.'' Martin.

''Your support encouraged me to have more confidence in a writing routine and to get the material I teach into written form.'' Lydia.

''You have provided an incredible foundation as a platform for my book going forward.'' Christine

''I was reluctant at first to start writing my book. With your encouragement, I remembered how writing helped me reclaim 'me' again. I can hardly stop!'' Susie

''Your processes work. Especially for someone who wishes to write a novel. You have certainly given me much food for thought. I shall be eternally grateful.'' Barbara

"Thanks, Wendy, for your fabulous teachings." Satminder

"The content shared has helped me get clear on the many areas of writing my book. I can wholeheartedly recommend journaling to anyone who seriously considers finally writing that book that has been calling them!" Deborah

"This book will advance your career. You will be in the very best set of hands. The author seriously helps you raise your game as a writer." Ann

"I highly recommend Wendy, her books and her services." Sasha

"I learned when I connected with my heart, the writing did flow. No halting or procrastination. Thank you for that, Wendy." Peggy

"Everything is easy with your uncomplicated guidance, thanks." Lara

"Thank you so much, Wendy, for your wealth of knowledge provided." Loretta

"Your books and your work are a shining example of a life put to productive use. I can't thank you enough." Jesse

"Your programme gave me the new perspective I needed to write and publish my first book. Thank you, Wendy." Jillian

''I have made many discoveries upon reading and utilising the content. One is the more you write, the easier it becomes, and you can even get faster at it.'' Bob

''With your support, I was able to express what's inside in the written sense. I gained insight and perspective for the content of my book. Thank you'' Lisa

YOUR INVITATION TO WRITE FROM YOUR HEART

Invitation

Thank you for joining me on this invitation to discover your author voice through journaling. On this ticket to ride, please know you have everything you need inside to write from your heart. Grab a pen and a notebook and let us get started on the adventure of a lifetime. A new chapter awaits.

Fill your paper with the breathings of your heart
- William Wordsworth

Foreword

Written by Anne Jirsch author of
Future Vision Your Working Life
10 Strategies to Help You Get Ahead

I loved Wendy Fry's first book. I noticed how it was easy to read, how the narrative drew me in and how it flowed. Later, when Wendy began helping budding writers, I recommended her services to various people. They have all remarked how well their books (now published) came together.

After writing five books myself, I know how easy it is to get bogged down or lost along the way. Wendy gives you the structure and shows you how to develop your writing in easy bite-size pieces.

At times we find ourselves holding back instead of telling our story. By journaling, we find the real you, the authentic you. With Wendy's guidance, your words will become magical.

In this book, you will discover how to 'own' your words, to develop your skill as a writer, and how to be brave. Yes, brave, brave enough to heard and to reveal the real you.

If you want to write on any level: a blog, book, journal or feature use this book as your personal guide and watch your words come alive and dance across the page.

Contents

Part Three

Part Four

Part Five

Part Six

Part Seven

Introduction

Write from Your Heart

Discover Your Author Voice Through Journaling

Introduction

You have a story to tell. A unique message to share. An authentic voice wanting to speak and be heard. Your story, your truth, The words of your heart matter. Now is the time to set them free.

The processes shared within Write from Your Heart will inspire you and teach you how to express yourself through a range of practical writing exercises and empower you to find your author voice.

Delightful prompts and writing invitations will encourage you to look forward to the journaling process and help you recognise the positive impact heart-centred journaling brings.

Imaginative ideas will teach you how to put pen to paper to grow into the habit of daily journaling to maximise your health, your relationships, your work and your life as a writer.

Now, you can break through limiting beliefs about your writing ability quickly and easily, saying no to writer's block and yes to understanding how to write for pleasure or as a professional author in any genre.

In Write from Your Heart, Writing Coach Wendy Fry offers a range of engaging writing invitations, inspiring prompts, and shares her author tips to support you in gaining confidence as a writer and sharing your story.

This easy to apply writing guide includes powerful principles to overcome the fear of writing, encouraging you to keep your name on the page and your words flowing.

You will gain the following benefits as you read through:

- ✓ **Tools and techniques to get you in *'The Write Frame of Mind'***
- ✓ **Journaling invitations to express your author voice confidently**
- ✓ **Guidance on how to feel comfortable unleashing the power of your truth**
- ✓ **Heart-centred exercises to revive a tired mind and body to create writers flow**
- ✓ **Prompts to write a better story for yourself**
- ✓ **Access to The Spotlight Process tapping into your innate creativity with confidence**
- ✓ **Topic ideas to keep you engaged on your writing journey**
- ✓ **Exercises for self-journaling and creative writing groups**
- ✓ **Processes to boost your writing flow**
- ✓ **Guidelines to support you in finding your preferred journaling style**
- ✓ **Writing invitations to aid personal transformation and healing**
- ✓ **Tips for integrating journaling into your daily routine**
- ✓ **Prompts to set your author voice free**

HOW TO USE THIS BOOK

Follow the exercises and writing prompts when you see this graphic.

Use your journal as a listening ear and set the words of your heart free. Write every day by hand in your journal or on loose-leaf paper. Write uncensored. Speak your truth. Care more about substance and less about style, grammar and punctuation.

Recognise the importance of journaling to discover your author voice. Your story and personal expression matter most on this journaling invitation

Who are you not to write? You have every right!

Now Is the Time to get right to the heart of the matter. It's time to step up and rise and shine as an author. Write from Your Heart will show you how.

"Being aware of the past is helpful. Living there isn't. Now is the time to get on with the joy of living and writing from your heart ~ Wendy Fry

About Wendy's Writing Journey

From an early age, I hated writing. As much as I tried, tongue sticking out in concentration, trying to remember the shape and the curve of each letter. My little fingers gripping a stubby pencil and saying 'bottoms' when I missed out sections of the alphabet or confused the letters back to front, I couldn't get it right. Perhaps you've been there too?

I dreaded having to recite the alphabet though I must admit, the *'L, M, N, O, P'* section was the most fun. Taking a deep breath in when I got to this part, puffing up my chest in a sing-song voice and waving my arms about as if I was conducting an orchestra, I always remembered the 'lemon part' as I called it!

Join me now, stand up, take a breath and in your best singing voice let's have a rendition of ''L, M, N, O, P'' and have a little shimmy with it if you must.

Grumpy, tearful and afraid of 'THE ALPHABET' which seemed as bad as saying a rude word and not knowing what it meant, I KNEW IT WAS BAD! I sat cross-legged, on the chocolate coloured carpet in the house I grew up in, 13 Milton Road, Wimbledon SW19 in despair. My chubby legs were full of pins and needles from lack of movement, surrounded by balls of scrunched up paper. Eyes streaming with tears and crying hysterically as my mother's angry face looked fit to burst because I couldn't learn the alphabet as quickly as she wanted me to.

The memory of her shouting and pointedly waving her index finger - *"you'll learn this bloody alphabet if it kills me*" in the confused mind of a four-year-old didn't I want to get it right in case it killed my mother. Subconsciously I was blocking myself from writing.

What do you remember about learning to read and write?

Was it a joyful experience or one which may have blocked you from achieving success as a writer?

You may like to write your account in your journal.

Turning Point Moment – Falling in Love with Writing

I was fifteen, neither a child, not an adult. In limbo-land. Part of me still wanting to play with Fuzzy Felts and Etch a Sketch and the other part, immersed in

Rimmel Twilight Teaser Lipstick, jumper dresses and heels I couldn't walk in. Crimped hair, Duran, Duran and 'Adam Ant' was calling me. As for boys, they were still stinky and yucky and yet there was a curiosity building.

My wake-up call to falling in love with writing freely from my heart was in secondary school when 'Mr Howard', the English Teacher at Sutton West set a homework essay to write on the topic *" My Family."* This writing project was BANG on time, and I couldn't wait to spew the contents of my heart. My parents were getting a DIVORCE. I had no idea what a DIVORCE was though it is sure as hell worse than THE ALPHABET!

Growing up was a confusing time for me. All that I had known had become unknown. I felt like a zombie, staggering about in a stunned daze.

I didn't tell a soul about how I was feeling. Instead, I wrote pages and pages about *My Family.* Pen and paper became my trusted friend.

Communicating in a new way without fear of judgement, blame or upsetting either parent while trying to make the best decision who I chose to live with, I wrote out my deepest hurts and fears.

I knew in that turning point moment, swinging on my wonky chair by the window in the English hut, 5B my life would never be the same because I'd fallen in love with writing. Writing truthfully about my heartfelt experiences was then and still is now totally freeing.

As a result of this life-changing poop storm, homework of the essay kind took on a new meaning and my writing ability improved prolifically. Not writing for reward or recognition, purely to release emotional pain, it was an unexpected bonus to receive A's in red pen for my English work. I nearly kissed Mr Howard for introducing me to 'writing from my heart', but he had an orange beard with some of his lunch attached and the overwhelming stale smell, I rapidly reigned in that idea. The man was a genius, a master in the making; he knew the power of words and how they can change lives. I am genuinely grateful for that day.

So, you see, *'My Story'* and my writing journey began out of shock, fear, confusion and uncertainty. I do believe writing from my heart saved my life and got me through those dark days.

My BIG WHY (the reason I write) is plain and simple. I write to **H**elp **O**ther **P**eople **E**volve. To encourage them to share their story and write from their hearts.

Be sure to share the words of your heart with your journal. Perhaps you will agree, it's about time you set your words free?

Here I am in the centre of the photo on school Mufti Day aged fifteen 'giving it large' with a group of fabulous girlfriends.

You are not what happened to you – YOU define who you become – Wendy Fry

PART ONE

FALL IN LOVE WITH WRITING FROM YOUR HEART

FALL IN LOVE WITH WRITING FROM YOUR HEART

The future starts when I wake up every morning. Every day I find something creative to do with my life - Miles Davis

Write from Your Heart – Discover your author voice through journaling is an invitation for you to record your thoughts, feelings and daily events writing about your life as it is or at how you remember it to be.

The writing prompts and exercises shared will help you understand your past, present and future exploring various journaling methodologies. When you stop shining the light on the past, you allow yourself to notice how bright your future is in the now.

Bring your curiosity along and notice the personal benefits you will gain when you write from your heart tearlessly. Journaling is the first step stone in sharing your voice and your evolution as an author.

Every day is a great day to fall in love with writing from your heart – Wendy Fry

BEGIN WITH THE END IN MIND

End of journal piece self-reflective questions

Invitation

Copy the following prompts into the front of your journal for easy reference

- ✓ **How will this journal piece support me as an author?**
- ✓ **What benefits did I gain from writing this journal entry?**
- ✓ **What did I find particularly interesting about this piece?**
- ✓ **What challenged me in writing about this topic?**
- ✓ **What have I learnt about myself personally or professionally in this piece of writing?**
- ✓ **Based on my experience and my journal entry, who else may benefit from reading my words?**
- ✓ **How can I best use my experience in the form of a book to inspire my reader?**

- ✓ **How is my life experience translatable into a critical message for those reading?**
- ✓ **What words of wisdom can I share as an author to help others heal, evolve and transform?**
- ✓ **What ideas and themes do I notice for future books, blogs and topics to share with my audience?**
- ✓ **What can I choose to do *now* do to make the rest of my day, evening, week, month or year ahead even better after considering what I have recorded?**

Write your dreams in a journal, notebook, or on a cork. When you pen down your dreams an inner strength and divine power is activated for you to work towards the fulfilment of your dreams - Lailah Gifty Akita

JOURNALING – HOW TO GET STARTED

What you need to get started:

A desire to make a positive change for yourself first and foremost.

- ✓ **This book**
- ✓ **Your amazing self**
- ✓ **Your Thoughts**
- ✓ **Your Heart**
- ✓ **A sense of curiosity**
- ✓ **Pen & paper**

Keep journaling simple: Pen and paper, journal, loose-leaf paper or notebook is all that's needed. You may wish to carry a pocketbook or diary around with you or by your bedside to make notes and journal entries when the writing mood hits, and I promise you, it will.

The more you write, the more you want to. In my experience, writing can be a healthy addiction, and you may find yourself reaching out for your journal as the best means of personal expression and support. Your journal is there for you when you wish to speak freely.

JOURNALING TIPS

I can't write to please everyone. But someone, somewhere, will be touched if I put my heart into it - Sara Winters

- Write every day (start with ten minutes and build up to twenty minutes or more)
- Make it easy (pen and paper or notebook)
- Write from your heart uncensored
- Care more about substance and less about style, grammar and punctuation
- Recognise the importance of journaling and how regular self-expression can improve your life

WORDS FROM THE HEART

A book isn't just a book; it's a chunk of someone's life you are holding in your hands. The author's heart and soul captured there between the pages. The blood, sweat and tears weaved into wisdom and shared to make your journey to becoming an author an easier one - Wendy Fry

I love learning about new words and concepts. Having not heard this expression before I became curious to discover the meaning of *'Hridaya'* which is a Sanskrit word and a term used to describe the spiritual heart and the energy contained within the heart chakra. The spiritual heart brings you to the centre of yourself. We have more impact and connectivity with each other than we may have realised.

Writing from my heart with love is at the core of my being. The title of this book came to me naturally through intuition as does much of my work, teachings and writing. I work in a heart centred way with my clients and delivering workshops and training courses to help them recognise how far they have come and how their hearts got them through when their minds struggled with the overwhelm of life.

Whatever life challenges you have overcome, the 'poop' you may be trying to wade through right now or your fears for the future, please know and remember, you carry the solution to any problem inside yourself.

I encourage you to use the exercises shared throughout this book to bring balance to your thinking and activate the words of your heart. In doing so, when you write uncensored, you learn about yourself and the world at large. Take time to understand your behaviours, stressors, emotions, thoughts, feelings and motivators.

Writing about the crud of life as well as the juicy and fun parts allows you to become more solution-focused than problem-centred.

You find many in roads and out roads through journaling which bring new opportunities and undiscovered horizons for writing opportunities. You may even find the thought of the uncertainty becomes exciting for you and welcome each new day knowing whatever happens you can handle it.

All changes, both the planned and shocking ones, require inner mastery. I am writing this book while amid a global crisis My hope is, with awareness, you too can adapt and gain flexibility when life is unknown and take one day at a time savouring the positives in life.

If you know, before starting this journey, you will benefit from my coaching and mentoring to include emotional support do reach out to discuss my range of support options. www.wendyfry.com

Those of you who have experienced trauma can finally move on from the past and re-write your future using the journaling process. Realise the past no longer needs to hold you back from becoming an author.

Side effects recorded by my private journaling case study clients are a noticeable improvement in relationships, assertive communication, improved confidence, understanding of self, clarity of thoughts, and noticing an increase in wellbeing. Those who write every day consistently felt happier, lighter and freer.

Without a ton of 'stuff' weighing you down, it's going to be interesting what you discover on this writing journey. Thank you for taking the time to share the positive benefits you notice from reading this book by leaving a review on an Amazon or contacting me directly at www.wendyfry.com

HISTORY OF JOURNALING

Writers Write. They notice the detail inside and outside of themselves. Writers use their senses at the deepest level. They write with guts, determination and motivation, most of all they write with their hearts and minds - Wendy Fry

The deliberate practice of writing has been traced back historically to some of the greatest influencers of all time. For centuries, keeping a diary, journal or record of events and having ones one's moods, experiences and memories have made history.

The many powerful quotes shared throughout Write from Your Heart inspire you to raise your game and think like an author.

This Journaling Invitation features the process of writing by hand for simplicity, though the history of writing is exciting and broad.

The world since the dawn of time has been full of writers and creatives expressing themselves in some form of written communication. This book will guide you through sharing your authentic voice and as an aspiring author supporting you to be confident to begin to want to share your book of words.

You may be interested in researching your ancestors and family history to discover the writers in your timeline and how you. You may choose to follow in their footsteps or indeed be the first in a long line of writers carving a writing career of your own.

Write from your heart includes some examples of powerful voices who have had their works documented. Notice how their use of words reaches you and educates you to think differently.

Scientists Charles Darwin and Isaac Newton's research and writings make for fabulous reading and insights. Ernest Hemingway and Leonardo Da Vinci are encouraging influencers.

Political figures Abraham Lincoln and Winston Churchill teach us much about the impact of words when writing and delivering speeches. Historical figure Marcus Aurelius spent time writing for pleasure.

Many of these change-makers have been vital influencers producing quotes and 'words of art' which have travelled with us through time—their impactful words leaving a positive legacy in our hearts and minds.

Scholars of various disciplines have found journaling to have many benefits, including psychological functioning, improvement in health and physical health advances (Smyth, 1998.)

Journaling for extended periods is said to gain improvements in emotional well-being (Park and Blumberg, 2002) Improvement in day-to-day mood (Paez et al., 1999) and reduction in symptoms of depression (Lepore, 1997)

Here are some of my favourite quotes:

"Imagination is more important than knowledge"
- Albert Einstein

"Writers are special people. Every person is a special kind of writer"
- Elsa Gidlow

"A writer is a world trapped in a person"
- Victor Hugo

"Real freedom is in one's heart, irrespective of external conditions"
- N. Sri Ram

"Carry your heart through this world like a life-giving sun"
- Hafez

"One open heart has the power to ignite many hearts"
- Chantelle Renee

"Write it on your heart that every day Is the best day of the year"
- Ralph Waldo Emerson

THE POWER OF WRITING FROM YOUR HEART

The heart has its reasons that reason cannot know - Blaise Pascal

The Heart's Natural Intelligence

No longer are we at the mercy of our minds alone. When we recall the emotions of our hearts and consider the deeper workings of this magical chamber which keeps us alive, we remember the words inside unspoken.

Inspirational speakers and research scientists are making huge leaps in understanding the heart as an intelligent organ as well as the emotive workings of our heartfelt experiences. I share in brief some of the most influential speakers and influencers working in the area of heart-based research.

Greg Braden, global speaker and author, indicates there is more communication being sent from the heart to the brain than being received from it. Greg has some fascinating books to study and talks available on YouTube if you too are interested in following his work and expanding your knowledge in this area.

Greg's teaching techniques using the heart as an intelligent educate, inform and in turn, raise consciousness awareness, I love his work and teachings. The HeartMath Institute offers the scientific angle of heart function, variability and research which encourages us to look at our heart in a completely new way to understand the heart are more than a mechanism bringing blood to our organs. HeartMath research explains the heart begins beating in an unborn foetus before the brain forms. Scientists call this process autorhythmic. This area of research fascinates me. The 'brain in the heart' has a complex system which we may not have previously understood. As humans, we form the emotional brain long before the rational mind I have been interested to learn.

The electromagnetic field of the heart is approximately 50,000 times stronger than the magnetic field of the brain and can be detected several feet away from the body with sensitive manometers. I've often wondered if this is how we naturally sense when something is wrong. If we follow our intuition and take a particular choice, we may choose to apply the hearts wisdom over and above gut instinct and rational choice.

In the second half of the 20th century, pioneer psychologists John and Beatrice Lacey researched the idea of the heart's intelligence-sharing insights into the live communications going on inside of us between heart and mind which we may never have imagined from our limited knowledge taking place. I love how when we understand the hearts intelligence how we can bring mind and body into balance and can begin to communicate by different means.

In 1991, pioneer Dr J. Andrew Amour introduced the term "heart brain." He shares insights and learnings, explaining the heart possesses a sophisticated and intrinsic nervous system which, in and of itself, is a brain.

The Institute of HeartMath details how thousands of people use the power of their hearts to improve their lives. In my work as a therapist, I believe this to be true. When we can manage our inner emotions, we can stabilise our heart and regulate our emotions, and in doing so, it becomes easier to manage our external worlds.

Tuning into our hearts to resolve problems and gain new insights is a new way of listening to our heart's innate intelligence.

HOW DOES JOURNALING WORK?

Dominant, hurtful emotions have less power on paper. By expressing our unique experiences through journaling, it will stop us feeling we are being eaten alive by our pasts, allowing us to get on with the business of living now. How will your life change when you write the story of your past and leave it there? - Wendy Fry

Journaling has many health and wellbeing benefits, but it doesn't stop there. As writers, if we get blocked on a writing a page, a chapter, back cover synopsis or in defining our unique message there is much we can do to support ourselves in writing our thoughts down by hand.

My best advice is if overwhelming emotions prevail in your life, journaling is one of the best ways to gain emotional catharsis and release the build-up of what is left unexpressed.

Releasing the thoughts of a busy mind frees up your focus and energy so you can get back to the business of writing from your heart.

BENEFITS OF JOURNALING

Listen. Make a way for yourself inside yourself - Rumi

Here are just a few of the general benefits to journaling

- Translates your emotional experiences onto paper
- Catalogues unspoken words bringing them into the physical world
- Used as an outlet to record thoughts, feelings and emotions as and when they occur or as a self-reflection tool
- Helps you understand your past, present and future thinking
- Connects you to discovering joy and gratitude in the present moment
- Supports you in writing about your life, hopes and dreams
- Honours your experience and authentic voice
- Journaling enables you to express how you think and feel without judgement or opinion
- Used as a tool to compare and measure progress over time
- External means of support and constant companion
- Changes perspective when journal entries are re-read and questions throughout applied

SCIENTIFIC BENEFITS OF JOURNALING

Dr James Pennebaker, an expert in the field of expressive writing, suggests the best way to accesses direct memory recall is to write by hand. Writing by hand enables you to get your thoughts out more quickly than by other writing means fully accessing your unique voice.

- Writing by hand is said to have a direct link to heart
- Journal writing is flexible and caters to left and right-brained people
- The writing process directs the intention and reticular activation process of the mind

Right Brain Functions (left-hand control and hemisphere) Responsible for the left-hand side of the body is generally he more artistic and creative side of the brain.

Responsible for: 3-D Forms, Creativity, Imagination, Insight, Music awareness, Art awareness, holistic thought, Intuition

Left Brain Functions (right-hand control and hemisphere) Responsible for the right side of the body, and generally the more logical and academic side of the brain.

Responsible for: Number skills, Analytical thinking, science and math, Logic, Language, Writers, Reasoning

Both sides of the brain have different functions, as outlined above. The left-hand side of the brain controls the right-hand side of the body, and likewise, the right-hand side of the body coordinates the left-hand side of the body both parts connected by the corpus callosum.

Various studies, one completed by the University of Washington in 2009 found children writing an essay by hand for ten minutes on pen and paper were faster at writing compared with those working on computers

For those interested in brain functions and what happens when we write, there are many research studies freely available which go beyond the scope and intention of this book.

MENTAL, PHYSICAL AND EMOTIONAL HEALTH BENEFITS OF JOURNALING

The writing process in an outlet for all kinds of emotional overwhelm. You can tell anything you like to your journal, and it won't bat an eyelid - Wendy Fry

In the book - Opening by Writing it Down: How expressive writing improves health and eases emotional pain (Third Edition), there is a summary by Pennebaker, and co-author Joshua M. Smith details a case study of two groups assigned a writing project. Participants blood samples were taken before and after the study to conclude the results. One group recorded their deepest thoughts, traumas and emotions and the other group to write on specific superficial topics. This new test led researchers to find, those who wrote about their feelings, traumas and deepest thoughts had enhanced immune function compared to those who wrote about superficial topics for the sake of writing.

Emotional upheaval touches every part of our lives. Losing a job or getting a divorce these two things affect all aspects of the relationship with others, our views of ourselves. Writing helps us focus and organise our life experiences and make sense of our worlds.

ANXIETY REDUCTION

When anxiety strikes, journaling enhances self-awareness, writing down your experiences and personal challenges also release pent up feelings.

Journaling about overwhelming emotions provides catharsis helping you let go of negative thoughts and everyday stresses along with your responses to them.

- **Help students to manage anxiety and stress as well as improve engagement and enhance meaning (Flinchbaugh, Moore, Chang & May 2012)**
- **Enables you to track your progress as you undergo treatment (Star, 2018)**
- **Reduces the physical symptoms of health problems, and anxiety in women (LaClaire, 2008)**
- **Reduces anxiety in patients with Multiple Sclerosis (Hasanzadeh, Khoshknab and Norozi, 2012)**

In an age where nearly everyone suffers anxiety to some degree and may not know how to best cope with overwhelming thoughts, emotions and experiences, you may like to share with your friends and colleagues the information, you are learning from this book in a way that's gentle and encouraging.

Saying something like '' do you know what I learned today'' opens a space for conversation to discuss using the journaling process and write from your heart as a strategy for general well-being. This way, the receiver of your communication may not take it as unwanted advice and may become curious about the benefits they may gain by journaling.

I wrote a social media post recently about the benefits of journaling in stressful times. Someone I don't know saw what I shared and contacted me directly to say the information I freely offered meant she turned to a journal to record her thoughts and feelings after her husband died. She didn't want to burden her friends or overwhelm her family who was also grieving and used the process of journaling to pour out her feelings of shock, loss and sadness as well as recording the love and the special memories shared. She wrote to me some months after her husband's passing to thank me for the post as it had helped her get through the times when she felt hopeless and alone. You never know how far your words may reach and how sharing them may help others heal.

When you share what inspires you from your heart and always with good intention, it can make a huge difference in someone else's life. The more people we help to manage their worlds through journaling, the better.

If you or anyone you know specifically want to read a supportive book to help you overcome anxiety. I recommend *'The Energy of Anxiety' by Ann Bowditch*. Available on Amazon.

EXPRESSIVE WRITING TO EASE DEPRESSION

Keeping a mood diary of thoughts, feelings, emotions and behaviours while experiencing depression has been known to boost mood and lessen the symptoms of negative emotions.

Focusing on and writing about what is going well boosts mood. Gratitude journaling also sees improvement in the reduction of depressive symptoms and duration of the problem.

Invitation

- ✓ **Begin the process of journaling freely writing by hand what comes into your mind or using the journaling prompts and exercises include in Write from Your heart**
- ✓ **Notice any repetitions of your thoughts, feelings, behaviours and emotions you record within your journal**
- ✓ **Reflect upon the benefits gained from journaling**

- ✓ **With new awareness, what positive changes and actions can you take toward creating a happier future for yourself?**
- ✓ **What have you noticed about your mood after journaling consistently for a minimum of 21 days?**

Early *HeartMath* research indicates heart rhythms become disordered and negative emotions throw the nervous system out of balance. Positive emotions found an increase in harmonious heart rhythms which, as well as reducing stress also enhanced improvement in world perceptions.

The following statistics indicate a research-based study.

- **People diagnosed with Major Depressive Disorder repeated significantly lower depression scores after three days of expressive writing for twenty minutes a day (Krpan, Kross, Berman, Deldin, Askren and Jondies, 2013)**
- **Expressive writing can reduce the symptoms of depression in women struggling with recovery from intimate partner violence (Koopman, Ismailji, Holmes, Classen, Palesh and Wales, 2005)**
- **Journaling may also be as effective as Cognitive Behavioural Therapy (CBT) for reducing symptoms of depression in high-**

risk adolescents (Stice, Burton, Bearman and Rhoode, 2006)

- **Expressive writing moderated the frequency of intrusive thoughts in depressed individuals leading to a reduction in symptoms (Lepoer, 1997)**
- **College students who are vulnerable to depression can help students with rumination and brooding, two known contributing factors of depressive symptoms (Gortner, Rude, and Pennebaker, 2006)**

GRATITUDE BENEFITS OF JOURNALING

There are a growing number of studies, self-help books and research based on the benefits of daily gratitude. Neuroscience reveals how gratitude rewires your brain to be happier. The nervous system is positively affected when writing about and stimulating feelings of happiness. UCLA's Mindfulness Awareness Research Centre suggests we feel healthier and happier when our brain focuses on positives. Gratitude transforms the molecular structure of the brain.

Cultivating the attitude of gratitude by written means is a useful tool for improving the quality of life and goal achievement. There are many ways to show appreciation Gratitude Journaling is just one way. I love this way of journaling and have kept gratitude diaries for many years.

A study designed to measure gratitude at the University of Miami which was conducted by Robert A. Emmons and Mike McCullough assigned three different journaling topics to randomly assigned participants. Each group was asked to write down their thoughts for ten weeks and either describe what was hassling them, write about their joys and what they were grateful for or keep track of neutral events.

The participants in the gratitude group revealed they felt twenty-five percent better than the other two groups. A later study by Emmons indicated keeping a gratitude journal enabled the people in that group to offer more emotional support to others in comparison to the other two groups.

- ✓ **According to (Seligman, Steen, Park and Peterson, 2005) Gratitude journaling makes you friendlier, more open and more likely to engage socially and increases your social support network**
- ✓ **Increase happiness and health as an indirect benefit by increasing optimism through writing with gratitude (Seligman, Steen, Park and Peterson, 2005)**
- ✓ **Boost long-term well-being, improve length and quality of sleep encourage exercise and reduce physical pain and symptoms through gratitude journaling (Emmons and McCullogh, 2003)**
- ✓ **Gratitude journaling is an aid to help you make progress toward your goals (Emmons and Mishra, 2011)**

As an aside of these studies, further research indicates journaling allows for the following breakthroughs to improve wellbeing.

Grief, Loss and Bereavement: Death of a loved one, personal loss and life-changing endings can be some of the most traumatic and heartbreaking events which journaling can help you through.

Writing about your symptoms of loss, grief and life-changing experiences help you to process your emotions and work through them. Research indicates the effectiveness of children dealing with bereavement through journaling (Kalantari, Yule, Dyregrov, Neshatdoost, and Ahmadi, 2012)

Recovery from addiction: Making a commitment to journal and holding yourself accountable for your progress as you overcome the challenges and personal struggles, as well as accomplishments associated with recovery from addiction, allows you to work through these circumstances, thoughts and feelings in a healthy manner (Milios, 2015)

Eating disorders and the people experiencing symptoms of or the medical diagnosis of such find writing in a daily diary can be a source of relief and inner healing. Writing about the associated problems, thoughts, feelings, symptoms and confronting problems in a journal can reduce the obsessive component of the disorder (Rabinor, 1991)

Traumatic events are experiences we may all go through at some time. What is traumatic for one may not be so for another person. Journaling can help to re-address the balance to help you notice the good in life and help you to see the positive side of experiencing trauma or indeed the gift in the situation once painful emotions are released. Journaling helps reduce the severe symptoms which can accompany trauma (Ullrich and Lutgendorf, 2002)

When coming to terms with a traumatic experience through journaling, writing for twenty minutes a day for three consecutive days indicates writing about the positive aspects of a traumatic experience was associated with the same benefits of writing about trauma (King and Milner (2000)

Improvements in well-being were gained by utilising the positive aspect of writing and looking for the gift in this situation and the positive outcome which may not have been evident at the time of the trauma.

IMPROVING WORKING MEMORY

Journaling can be helpful for those experiencing a history of trauma or PTSD. Writing enhances mental health and supports in aiding to process difficult events and negative emotions associated with traumatic memories. (Baikie & Wilhelm, 2005)

Writing can make us more self-aware and guides us to recognise unhealthy thoughts, patterns and behaviours. Putting things into perspective through writing and re-gaining or learning a sense of control aids in transforming a negative mindset to a positive one, especially about ourselves (Robinson, 2017)

Invitation

Baikie & Wilhelm (2005) offer the following tips to ensure journaling is constructive and works towards improving mental health symptoms to ease depression and increase well-being:

1. **Write in a private space keeping distractions to a minimum**
2. **Write at least once a day, every day. Ideally three to four times a day**
3. **Reflect on your writing and regain a sense of balance**

4. **Journal about what feels right for you now if you are journaling to overcome trauma (you do not need to write about the trauma event itself)**
5. **Structure your writing however it feels right to you**
6. **Keep your journal private unless you are working with a therapist or medical professional and have agreed to discuss your journal as part of your support plan**

Self-care: For painful, deeply traumatic memories which may surface as you write you may benefit from having a therapist, coach, emotional or mental health support practitioner to guide you for the duration or after completion of this book. You are welcome to make contact with the author if you would like to check on her availability to work with you therapeutically.

Wendy's has a background as a holistic therapist working in the wellbeing industry for over twenty years and has enabled her to test various methods across a range of problems. She has developed a choice of coaching & mentoring support programmes explicitly tailored to your needs on booking any programme.

www.wendyfry.com

PHYSICAL HEALTH BENEFITS

There are numerous research-based studies and examples of physical as well as mental and emotional benefits to journaling. I've listed a small sample below. You may also like to consider setting up a journaling group with friends, family or in your local community to explore collectively the group benefits gained through writing.

- **Immune system function improves by continually journaling about personal and emotional topics (Petrie et al., 2004)**
- **Fewer visits to the hospital (King and Miner, 2000)**
- **Liver function improvement (Francis and Pennebaker, 1992)**
- **Lung function improved with time ((Smyth et al., 1999)**
- **Blood pressure regulates (Davidson et al., 2002)**
- **Heart health rate changes (electrodermal activity and muscular activity (Pennebaker, 1997)**

If you are currently experiencing a mental or physical health diagnosis, consult your doctor, physician or mental health team if you have any concerns about using journaling as part of your treatment plan.

PART TWO

CHANGE YOUR LIFE THROUGH JOURNALING

YOU HAVE THE POWER TO CHANGE YOUR LIFE THROUGH JOURNALING

Your words have power. When you write freely from your heart, you will discover your author voice within. You can change your life through writing – Wendy Fry

Whether you write first thing in the morning, before sleeping at night, on the train or while waiting to pick your children up from school, always make time to write.

Find time in your lunch break, locked in the toilet, by torchlight under your bed covers, or discover a delightful place in nature to write and be inspired. You will find writing becomes a healthy addiction. You can't get enough of it.

There are many benefits to sharing the words of your heart. Here are a few of my top tips when it comes to writing.

1. **You learn to write by writing**
2. **Write regularly**
3. **Write uncensored**
4. **Write freely leaving editing and punctuation to the end**
5. **Imagine your end goal is already achieved and think, act and speak like an author**

6. **Use your journal to express your voice and share what needs to be said**
7. **Find out what you want to write about**
8. **What's your vision, your end goal, your motivation to write? Take Inspired action and write about what you love**
9. **Keep a journal at home and by your bedside**
10. **Take a notebook or pen and paper with you wherever you go**
11. **Make lists or bullet points for speed and ease**
12. **Write letters you don't send to release emotion**
13. **Compose poetry and prose**
14. **Scrawl ideas on the back of napkins and beer mats**
15. **Doodle ideas visually and then write about them**
16. **Sketch, paint, create something and then write about it**
17. **Use your favourite mood-boosting techniques to get in the 'write frame of mind.'**

Raise your energy by doing the things you love before you write.

There are many ways to improve writing flow. My personal favourites are Qi Gong, dancing, gardening, music, walking, and listening to upbeat music.

LIVING WITH PURPOSE

There is no greater agony than bearing an untold story inside you - Maya Angelou

Use the following writing exercise to explore who you are as an individual in your own right.

Invitation

Use the following prompts to explore deeply explore your unique self. Write your answers in your journal spending time to complete or coming back to each prompt to add more details as the information flows to you.

- Who am I?
- Who am I beyond my name?
- Who am I beyond my role as an author, daughter, sister, mother, aunt, father, son, brother, uncle, husband, employee, carer, provider etc
- What are my positive character traits? (i.e. empathic, loyal, patient, understanding, humorous etc.)

- What persona (mask) do I portray to the outside world: friends, strangers, partners, others?
- When am I not being real, honest and authentic with myself or others?
- If I were to be all of who I am unashamed, what would I reveal which I have up until now, kept hidden?
- By being more of who I am and less of who I'm not, how will this benefit me? (i.e. full self-expression, confidence, self-acceptance, pride in self, new beginnings, freedom from the past etc.)
- What actions can I take today and every day, which allows me to show the world who I am?

''When you are true to yourself, you can express all of who you are, holding nothing back. By doing so, you gain a sense of self-acceptance and confidence. As a writer and author, this is part of the journey of daring to be you, being brave enough to be real and sharing your story. '' Wendy Fry

This adapted excerpt is from Chapter Five. 'Living with Purpose' taken from my second book Mothers and Daughters

UNSENT LETTERS, PAST, PRESENT AND FUTURE

People start to heal the moment they feel heard - Cheryl Richardson

You have the power to change your life through writing.

Your past need not negatively determine your future. Wisdom and learning based on your personal experiences can be shared in the written form and used for self-healing or indeed to inspire your readers to move past the past because that's not where the future is.

It's never too late to start writing and journaling from your heart to create a different future.

If we let it, our past determines our future negatively. Unless we explore how we remember it and what happened to us and examine the limiting beliefs and judgements, we place on ourselves or others because of those experiences we may never grow into our full potential - Wendy Fry

INCREASE YOUR HAPPINESS THROUGH JOURNALING

Journaling helps you at the deepest level to share your story and voice your thoughts, feelings, joys, hopes and fears. A place to record the innermost workings of your heart and mind - Wendy Fry

Simple Pleasures Make Me Smile Exercise

I love this exercise, and it's one of my favourite experiences as it is such a simple and easy process to boost happiness and get you into the writing flow

1. Read through the exercise slowly, savouring each part
2. Take your hands to your heart centre as shown in the diagram or if you prefer to rest your hands gently over your physical heart centre one on top of the other
3. Take your mind to someone or something you love?

4. When you think about the person or thing which popped into your mind, make a mental note of what you are experiencing.
5. Feel the love and connection in your heart space. What does that feel like for you?
6. What can you see visually in your mind's eye?
7. What do you hear - be aware of the sounds?
8. What smells come to your awareness?
9. What do you taste and sense from having this re-lived moment?
10. Make the picture brighter, stronger, sharper, more precise. Turn up the feelings, expand them, enjoy then, allow them to run throughout your body. Switch up the sounds, make them louder, more melodic, freeing. Sharpen your senses, your taste and smells. Savour the moment and notice your inner and outer smile.
11. Write about your experience of this exercise in your journal
12. If you sketch or paint you may like to express this experience in at form too

This exercise is beautiful, especially if you are feeling unloved, lost or afraid, missing a loved one, a pet, or feeling uncertain, alone or in despair. There are many ways to adapt the exercise and indeed deepen it.

You can also explore if you wish taking energy from nature, sunlight, a body of water, colour or a photograph of a beautiful memory. Primarily the portal in which we travel through to access the ability to write from our hearts is first the hearts energy and then the mind. The more you practice heart-centred focus, the easier it becomes.

As a reminder, when we write about what we are grateful for including accessing positive memories, there are many benefits in keeping the attitude of gratitude which in turn makes us feel happier and more vibrant.

POSITIVE JOURNALING

Each time I write, I reaffirm my soul - Rob Bignall

I love this topic idea to boost mood and improve wellbeing writing about our powerful positive moments. It's beneficial to talk about and voice these experiences too.

I invite you to share your most profound sensory experiences with your journal. Notice your memories, your experience in the now, your future imaginings. Record the visuals, smells, sounds, scents, tastes. Write about what you sensed and your innermost feelings. Make notes about the meanings and beliefs you gained from those experiences.

You may decide to set up a journaling and writing group using Write from Your Heart, and the exercises included as part of your book club. This exercise is a fantastic way to get the group started asking each member to talk for a few minutes about their most positive memory.

Tell your story, in your words. Convey your joy, your love, your happiness, your hopes and dreams.

As I write these words to share with you, I feel energy rising in me. There have been many positive moments in my life, and I know there have been in yours too. Continue to reflect on your positive moments, your successes and your wins and achievements. Look for positives as you go through life and you will find them. Write about them in your journal from your heart. Express them freely.

For bulk orders of fifty or more copies of Write from Your Heart for your book club or book, writing events make contact the author enquire about discounts www.wendfry.com

WELL FORMED OUTCOMES

You have everything you need inside to tell your story - Wendy Fry

Use the following prompts to set your journaling and writing goals.

It's useful to use this process on any area of your life. Most of the questions will help you to get clear on the outcomes you wish to achieve, and the action steps you will need to take to get you to where you want to be.

Invitation

1. What do you want to achieve? Stated in positive terms
2. How will you know when you've got it? What will you see, hear, feel, smell, taste and sense?
3. When, where and with whom do you WANT this result?
4. When, where and with whom do you NOT WANT this result?
5. What resources do you already have to achieve this?

6. What additional resources do you need to support you to achieve the outcome?
7. What will happen when you achieve the results you WANT?
8. How will getting these results benefit you or others?
9. Do you want this change in any other situations?
10. How <u>will</u> making this change affect other areas of your life?
11. What <u>would</u> happen if you <u>did</u> make that change?
12. What <u>would</u> happen if you <u>didn't</u> make that change?
13. What <u>wouldn't</u> happen if you <u>did</u> make this change?
14. What <u>wouldn't</u> happen if you <u>didn't</u> make that change?
15. With this awareness, what's the first action you can take in the direction of your dreams?
16. What's the one thing you CAN DO TODAY, which will ultimately change the course of the choices you make?
17. Write about what you wish for has already come to pass taking yourself forward in time by six months, one year, three years, five years and ten years. From each point in time, what would your future self-advice you to stop doing, start doing or do differently?

WRITING BY HAND & EXPLORING CREATIVE PLAY

It's in your hands. Write your way to becoming an author - Wendy Fry

Writing in a journal activates the narrator function of our minds. Writing down our account of a challenging experience can lower psychological reactivity and increase our sense of well-being, even if we never show what we have written to anyone else.

Your handwriting is personal and intimate in the same way your voice and fingerprint is unique. In my work as a therapist, it never ceases to amaze me how much fun adults can have when they bring the play to writing. Whether its finger painting their words, conducting a 'word' orchestra, writing with pasta shapes or writing words within their handprints, when we 'play with energy' writing can seriously be a lot of fun.

It's interesting too, to compare your hands to your family's hand shape, size, texture, palms and fingerprints. My hands are the same shape and size as my mother's hands as opposed to resembling my fathers. My nephew's hands are taking the form of my bothers.

HELPING HANDS

Invitation

When was the last time you looked and your hands for the first time?

Have you ever studied them?

Write about your hands in your journal, the shape, texture, colour, lines, blemishes and scars.

Your hands are unique.

What do your hands provide you with daily?

How do your hands help you in your work or for pleasure?

Who benefits from the use of your hands?

When do you use your hands to help, heal or soothe others?

Take time today to notice your hands.

Write about your hands and how you've used your hands through time.

You may wish to draw around your hands and write some content inside of the outline.

Use this Journaling Invitation to ‘give you a hand’ in guiding you to write for your life from your heart.

Remember to give thanks to your beautiful hands and all they do for you.

HEART SPEAK

Invitation

Allow your heart to speak through the voice of your journal. Use my example as a basis if you wish to.

How do you want your journal to greet you?

What words of support and encouragement do you want to hear?

This is Your Journal Speaking

ALL your life

I mean ALL of it

Is welcome here

A place to share your hopes

Your dreams

Your fears

A haven to unburden yourself

To share your authentic voice

Perhaps for the first time

And not the last

Share with me your

Disappointments
Tell me of your heartbreak
Speak of your grief
Release your guilt
Reveal your shame
Unleash your anger
Express you pain
Those unspoken things
The events
Which you have never shared
Please tell me
I am here
Listening
Deeply
Be ALL of who you are
With me
Because you can
It's okay
I'm here for you
On those dark nights
Of your soul
I want to know
What keeps you awake at night
Share
ALL of it

I will listen deeply
Without judgement
I will support you
Until your tears
And words are spent
Time and time again
You can visit me
You can stop by
When it suits you
We can share a cup of tea
I have your favourite biscuits in
Please know
I am here for you 24/7
When others fail you
Which is natural for humans
We can leave
Those people
To do their best
And we can
Get down to the business of writing
I will share with you
My truth
I want you to know
I, as your journal
I will not lead you astray

I will not disappoint you
I will not hurt you
I will not shout or tell you to be quiet
I can't promise
I will not make you cry
Tears are good
Let them flow
Little one
I'm here for you
I will listen
I will support
I will hold you
Gently
I will be Whoever or whatever you want me to be
As your journal
There is no limit to what I can
Do for you
Even when you let go of yourself
I am holding you
Know my words are true
I will be here for you
When you need me
Always
When you think
ALL is said and done

And you move on with your life
I will wait patiently for you
To begin again
Anew
Whenever you need me
I am here
For you
The time has come dear friend
To write from your heart
And share
ALL of who you are
With me

PART THREE

WRITE WITH AN OPEN HEART

WRITE WITH AN OPEN HEART

The Heart Quadrant - what does my heart need?

Invitation

Ask yourself ''what does my heart need to express right now?'' and listen as to how it answers. Ask again, ''even deeper, what message does my heart want to share?''

Being aware of the authentic voice of your heart with the freedom to speak through journaling is a huge turning point when it gets down to the business of writing.

Consider your unmet needs from childhood. What did your younger self want to say which they didn't voice or expressed which was left unheard of fell on 'deaf ears?'

It's never too late to meet those needs now as an adult and write from your heart to your younger self with love, encouragement and support.

Our future selves too often need a boost, a champion to say ''hey you can do it, you've got what it takes, go for it, I have your back.'' Journaling to and from your future self can be a lot of fun too, especially when you're the cheerleader in your own life.

Sometimes, when we lose connection with our hearts. We go into our heads looking outside of ourselves for something or someone to fill us up what we believe is missing. Like a void or a gaping hole, we search for something to complete us. Instead, look within and express the voice of your heart and discover your authentic voice through journaling.

Copy out the picture of heart quadrant in your journal or on pieces of paper.

Alternatively, you may like to purchase a heart-shaped note pad or make your hearts from different coloured papers and gift wrap or card.

Write inside your heart-shaped flower petals, what your heart needs to express. You may have never even stopped to think about what your heart needs, and this is the best way for you to discover your authentic voice and the voice of your heart.

After completing, next write out either on the back of the heart, in your journal or some new hearts, all the choices, affirmations, loving statements and acknowledgements which make you feel warm and lovable.

Completing this exercise daily on waking and sleeping as well as throughout the day in your journal or on the heart shapes will have a dramatic effect on your ability to openly express yourself and in turn improve your inner and outer communications.

MY HEART SAYS YES. MY HEAD SAYS NO

Head and heart can conflict at different times, two parts of you in disagreement, battling with each other for pole position. Have you found yourself unable to make decisions based on that inner conflict, not knowing which way to go?

A question I would like you to become familiar with is:

'Am I in my head, or am I in my heart?'

Often, we are in our heads to the absence of listening to heart-centred communication and discovering our authentic inner voice. Many wouldn't recognise it if it came up and stared us in the face.

Our heads analyse and we, weigh up the pros and cons of a situation. It's where our voice of doom lives and rears its ugly head until we rein it in. If we're not careful, we could let our heads rule our hearts and our future, never considering the heart's needs or wants. It's time to start again and to write a new chapter and future into being.

OPENING YOUR HEART

An open and expressive heart is mighty powerful.

- **Your heart is wise**
- **If you listen to it, you will find that it knows all the answers to all your questions**
- **Your heart provides you with valuable sources of information**
- **Your heart has a blueprint for happiness, joy and compassion for yourself and others**
- **Your heart stores that which you seek**
- **Your heart if you listen to it will tell you what it wants to say, what it wants to share and why sharing its message will have a profound impact on your ability as a writer and generally living life to your maximum potential**

The heart is where our true self resides, that place of inner knowing and intuition, the higher self, the source, our oneness.

Following your heart in the journaling process supports you in discovering your unique voice and connecting with the writer within.

Now is the perfect time to write, when we let go of the past and move forward into the unknown and writing what comes through from our hearts message, we grow magnificently and in doing so step fully into our power.

Heart Speak Writing Invitation

- Listen to your heart's needs
- Be aware of the fears in your head
- Make a note of where these fears come from Are they fear from the past, current concerns or worries about things you imagine happening in the future?
- When you think about your fears, who comes to mind, how do you feel physiologically?
- Bring yourself back to your heart each time you find yourself going back into your head
- Go back to the heart and ask yourself 'what does my heart want to say'
- What does my heart need to feel?
- With the wisdom of my heart, what is the journal piece I must write?
- Act and write from your heart in every situation

In my experience, being a writer is about being fearless; when you write and speak from your heart, you discover freedom.

May your choices reflect your hopes, not your fears
– Nelson Mandela

PAST POSITIVES AND WONDERFUL FUTURES

Our hearts and minds are amazing if we use them to our best advantage. We have a storehouse of information deep inside which we can access whenever we want and wherever we are - Wendy Fry

Writing your experiences in the positive tense has many benefits as this book exemplifies. This beautiful heart-centred exercise will support you to connect in and then outwardly communicate the words of your heart through your journal.

Past Positives Invitation

1. Place your hand's palm to palm, directly over the centre of your chest fingers extending to your heart, laying one hand flat on top of the other and take deep breaths in and out. Laying on of your hands on your physical body, thus 'the energy body' helps to not only stabilise the heart it also connects you with your heart's innate intelligence and information centre.

2. Slow down your breathing, taking nice, deep and easy breaths taking the breath down to

your stomach area. When breathing in this way and slowing down your breathing, you stimulate the relaxation response. A deeper breath can be noted by your stomach, which will expand on breathing in and on breathing out decrease the distension. Breathing this way has many health as well as emotional benefits.

3. Take your heart and mind to a beautiful memory in time and space to a place where you felt/feel happy and positive
4. What do you notice?
5. Where are/were you?
6. What is/was the event or occasion?
7. Were you alone or with others?
8. What was the time of day, the month year?
9. What do/did you see, hear, feel, smell, taste and sense?
10. Turn those senses up
11. Continue to take some deep breaths in and out
12. Allow the sensory experience to rise within you
13. Remember the 'data energy' the information which comes back to you which is in your internal storage system of thoughts, feelings, emotions and senses - enjoy!

14. Repeat as and when needed.

15. It's lovely to write about your positive memories and future positive projections in your journal in detail. Access positive memories and regenerate the feelings of joy, bliss, happiness through journaling or project yourself into the future seeing positive outcomes as you move on from any current setbacks and challenges

WHAT'S YOUR WHY – WHY DO YOU WANT TO WRITE?

Writing a journal reminds you of your goals and of your learning in life. It offers a place where you can deliberate, thoughtful conversation with yourself - Robin S. Sharma

For journal writing, at this point, you may not be writing to have your journal read, turned into a book, published or self-published, to make money or shared in any way. Right now, you may be writing for any of the following reasons

- **Writing for enjoyment**
- **Writing to heal**
- **Personal reflection**
- **Expressing your truth**
- **EducatingRecording life experience**
- **Catharsis**
- **Overcoming difficulties**
- **Self-expression**
- **Get in the habit of writing**
- **Gain clarity and insight**
- **Understand patterns and behaviours**
- **Write your first book or complete the one you've started**

Consider why you are reading this book and what your end goal is. How will journaling help you to achieve your goal step by step from where you are now?

Write down your reasons to write in your journal.

If you are using this book intending to write a book or book series, you may wish to extend this writing piece and detail:

- ✓ Your ideal day when you are writing your book
- ✓ What it feels like to have your book published or self-published
- ✓ Detail how your book has helped you to start a business or raise your professional status
- ✓ Write a business plan as to how you intend to apply writing and speaking from your heart in your daily life.

WRITING TIPS AND PROMPTS

Share your unique voice in your journal. Become the writer only you can be. Write from your heart freely - Wendy Fry

- Write every day by hand in your journal or on loose-leaf paper (start with five minutes and build up to twenty to thirty minutes or more if you choose to make more time for you)
- Make it easy (pen, paper, notebook or diary)
- Write from your heart uncensored, speak your truth
- For fun, with your non-dominant hand to access a deeper level of communication and to connect with the 'inner child.' When we write this way, we allow our younger selves to express what they may never have had the opportunity to share
- Care more about substance and less about style, grammar and punctuation. Your story and personal expression matter most on this journaling invitation
- Recognise the importance of journaling and how regular self-expression can improve your life in so many beautiful ways

DISCOVER YOUR AUTHOR VOICE

If you want to get on with your life, write the story of your past and leave it there - Wendy Fry

What's Your Story? Rewriting your history – Transforming your future

Your life tells a story, and there is someone out there who needs to hear it. You may think your story is not sensational, but it does not have to be sensational. It just has to be sincere. If your audience can relate to you and your experiences, and chances are they will, then you need to tell what you have been through, share your life, share your love and share your message with the world - Mark Brown 1995 World Champion public speaker.

I used to question 'why me?' Why do good things happen to bad people and no matter how hard I try, life throws continual curve balls which knock me down and every time I got back up, bam, I would be knocked back down. Nothing made sense to me. Perhaps you too have had the same questions or got to the point where you need to make a significant change in your life?

I know my old stories chapter and verse, inside out. I used to share those accounts of life's furballs choking the life out of me at any given opportunity. My negative experiences became my comfort zone, my identity, my go-to story, which I knew so well. When I told these stories, it was like a bad case of the farts; everyone got a waft of it. Phewwww. Are you farting on everyone, and how does it serve you?

Let's cut to the chase. What story have you been telling others about your past? The detail of your experiences which you share on first meeting What do you share about your abilities and strengths. Hopes, dreams, Joys?

On those dark days when you retreat inside, how do you put yourself down? What behaviours make you unkind to yourself?

Now is the time to question your beliefs and recognise the outdated ones which may be limiting you and your success as you know it to be.

How will changing the meaning you place on the experience of your story serve you?

You are not your story. You are not what happened to you. You are what you choose to become.

What story are you telling?

How long have you been sharing this story?

What part of your experience is hindering you?

What have you learnt from living your life story?

Write your story one last time in such a way; you can be free from it

How can you use your experience of your past positively?

What gains and personal wins have you benefitted from because of your journey so far?

What is your new life story?

How do you want your story to end?

What positive legacy in the written or spoken word do you intend to leave behind?

Today is the first day of the rest of your life. How can you change your story to make it work for you and in turn, use your experiences to help others to heal, transform and excel?

SHARE THE VOICE OF YOUR HEART

Don't die with your story inside – set it free and live your life on purpose! - Wendy Fry

Have you heard the saying ''what doesn't kill you makes you stronger?

Real-life isn't always kind. Anyone can experience a setback, an overwhelming challenge or something which takes us off the course of action we had planned.

In times of stress, in my life experience as a writing coach, mentor and therapist I've listened to people pour out their hearts and break down saying *''Life Sucks,"* and *''Stop the ride I want to get off"* or worse still, ''*I can't take it anymore."* The information shared in Write from Your Heart will support you in exploring your thinking concerning life's stressors and to question is life as bad as you think it to be?

All those worries, fears and imaginings. How much of that mountain of stress came true? All that anxiety you put yourself through – for what? Time wasted worrying about *'what if'* this, that or the other happens when there is no evidence it will come true except in your thinking?

A slice of Life Writing Invitation

Use the following writing exercise for self-reflection purposes. Writing about your life as it has been or how you remember it provides catharsis and is an opportunity to express your life experiences to date. Often, it's not until we start writing we realise there is much hurt still trapped within. By writing freely in our journals what we have lived through, we can heal at a deeper level and truly express the voice of our hearts.

Invitation

- **What's your catchphrase when life takes you down, and the going gets tough?**
- **Write about a time in your life when you were in fear or stressed about a specific experience or imagined outcome**
- **Perhaps right now, you're dealing with issues you hadn't foreseen, and the pressure is building up – write about it.**
- **Write about your experiences freehand in a journal express what it feels like to be living real life when it's in its most raw form.**

- **What keeps you awake at night?**
- **Write these things down before you go to sleep for emotional release**

In addition to writing about life's challenges as and when they hit, it will also support you to write about your inner strengths detailing how you moved beyond past setbacks.

FOR EVERY PROBLEM THERE IS A SOLUTION

Did you know, you can write words of encouragement from your 'future self' to the you that's sitting there reading these words right now? It's easy to write this way, try it and see. Write from the future perspective looking back to now. Write through the aspect of you who has moved beyond today's challenges.

'Future you' perspectives are generally loving, nurturing and understanding speaking in a compassionate and way through the voice of the heart.

What reassuring words do you need to hear right now? Write them down.

My favourite mantras are listed here below:

- Everything will be okay in the end.
- You are here right now, and It's okay. You're going to be okay.
- Where you're at right now isn't the end. It's a phase you are going through.
- This too will pass.

Life is precious, and we are truly blessed to be here. We may forget, at times, to enjoy life and find happiness no matter how small when everything seems overwhelming. Life *is* worth celebrating. We must remember to stop and pause.

Take a moment. Join me right now. Stop. Slow your breathing down. Take nice, deep and easy breaths in and out, again. Repeat. Notice you are still breathing – amazing. You can even laugh if you want to. Give thanks to you. A moment of self-appreciation. A pat on the back. A smile of acknowledgement. After all, look how far you've come. I am in awe of you!

LIVING TO TELL THE TALE

Invitation

Use the following writing prompts to support you in sharing your personal story. You may find by answering the points posed you find within your journal many book titles of ideas for blogs and sharing your author voice.

In my writing retreats, I ask those attending to use coloured highlighters to read through and highlight title ideas which would make a great book.

You will find when you write daily words on advertisements and in the media etc. offer you creative stimulation that will trigger your ideas for writing content.

- ✓ **How has your life experience shaped you for your greater good?**
- ✓ **If your life to date was a book title, what would you call it?**
- ✓ **What have you overcome despite your experiences and your imagined fears?**

- ✓ **How did you manage to overcome them?**
- ✓ **What makes you grateful to have the life you are now living?**
- ✓ **How did you get this far?**
- ✓ **What is your best advice to someone who has gone through or is currently going through your experience?**
- ✓ **What's your new motto for life in hindsight of what you've learnt and overcome?**

My favourite saying when the going gets tough is *'Bring it on. What's the best that can happen?"*

When you write from your heart freehand the process of handwriting in and of itself can be cathartic, energising, motivating and inspiring. I often journal about the *'busyness'* of life to release the emotional build-up when I feel overwhelmed with my to-do list.

I write about my choices in life and recognise the part I play when things get on top of me allowing me to reflect on what I'm saying yes to which gets in the way of what I want to do.

Journaling helps me to prioritise and plan ahead to focus on what's essential for my next day, week, month and year ahead.

It's also fun to write about forthcoming events I am looking forward to attending. I journal about the projects I am working on and what I want to create. I love nothing better than using my journal as a reflection tool and record the happy moments in my day or indeed to write about past experiences which have given me much joy.

You may notice as your momentum to write every day increases you build resilience and become more confident with writing freely.

'A problem shared is a problem halved,' so says an old wife's tale. If there is no one to listen to what you know you must share or else you will metaphorically explode, please know your journal will always be there for you, ready to support you with a listening ear.

Your journal may be the friend you have waited your whole life to confide in who will love, honour and accept you for who you are. Be curious to explore how forming this new relationship will benefit you as you notice your life-changing positively.

I believe each one of us is a natural storyteller. We each can write and speak from the heart once we know how to. Your journal will support you not only to heal though also to guide you to discover your authentic author voice.

You may like to write about your family and friends, your health, relationships, career, personal hobbies, money & finance, personal or spiritual development, your home and environment. There is no limit to what once you can write. I'm curious as to what you focus on, which will ignite your writing passion and how writing will support you in creating a beautiful feature for yourself.

If life gets' tough, and you know you will benefit from my support with the emotional as well as planning and content side of writing do contact me to check on my availability to support you in getting to the heart of the matter. I'm here to assist you in working through those everyday writing problems and issues of the heart. www.wendyfry.com

SEVENTY JOURNALING TYPES

Powerful, hurtful emotions have less power on paper. By expressing our unique experiences, it will stop us feeling we are being eaten alive by our pasts and we can get on with writing from the heart - Wendy Fry

My goodness. While researching journaling processes, types and preferences, I learnt a thing or three. I love the journaling ideas I've discovered which I'm sharing here with you.

There is no right way to journal, and my best advice is to try out a variety of ideas. Consider changing your journaling style every twenty-one days, monthly or seasonally and explore the best fit for you.

If you lose motivation, notice you stop journaling or don't find the time to give your journal your full commitment, chose a quick and easy journaling option from the list as an alternative.

In no specific order here are some lovey journaling prompts to get you started:

1. **Gratitude Journaling. 'Today I am grateful for' (list all the things, people and experiences you are grateful for each day)**
2. **Greeting the Day or Greeting the Night Journal (writing down your intention or positive affirmation for your day or evening ahead)**

3. **Self-care Journaling - Journal to the self (your daily personal dedication), i.e. 'I could take better care of myself today by' (add your call to action here)**

4. **Daily Diary - Daily Reflections Journal. I call this The Three W's. Ask yourself - What Went Well? What can I do to make tomorrow even better?**

5. **Daily Mind Dump - Writing freely and releasing all stressors and overwhelming emotions. I share this activity with all new clients to help them release the emotional build-up they have held onto before they get to the point of working with me**

6. **Prompt Journaling – can be about anything you are inspired and motivated to write. There are examples throughout this book**

7. **Writing from Life - Simply recording what you notice from your own life and the lives of others**

8. **Thoughts and Feelings (Mood Journaling) - Record and track thoughts and feelings as you go through your day**

9. **Morning Pages - Writing on three sides of A4 paper each morning (this idea comes from Julia Cameron's book, The Artists Way)**

10. **Mindfulness Journaling - what you notice in the present moment (what do you see, hear, feel, smell, taste, and what do you sense?)**

11. **Idea Journaling - Jotting down your ideas for creative projects, your bucket list, DIY and home repair, book titles you will write, recipe ideas etc**

12. **Intuitive Journaling – Record your insights and messages**

13. **Goal and Actions Journaling – Record what you wish to achieve. Include the date you want to complete your end goal and the times on which you will take action towards your goal. You can use this process on all areas of your life (writing and becoming an author, health, relationships, career, relationships etc.)**

14. **Bullet Journaling – This quick and easy journaling process is by far the simplest way to journal. Writing about whatever you wish to start with a bullet point. I adapt this exercise using hearts stars, funny faces, exclamation marks and hashtags. You may like to purchase some fun colour pens for different topics journaled**

15. **Health Journal (recording your nutrition, mobility, medical or dental treatment, mental, emotional health, emotional health day-to-day) Releasing emotions through journaling as your health or the health of a loved one changes can be deeply cathartic**

16. **Spontaneous Journaling – Change your writing topic as you go and write about anything and everything as the mood takes**

17. **Personal Sensory Journal – what did you see, hear, feel, smell, taste and sense today which inspired positive thoughts, feelings and emotions?**

18. **No Rules Journaling – write about whatever you want to and make it up as you go along.**

19. **Heart Quadrant Writing and Journaling**

20. **F**k It Journaling and other profanities. Take a deep breath in and on the out-breath to write down the things, people, situations, past event or future fear that's f* *king you off, (remember to keep breathing as you go along) make some noises with your mouth and lips too, it's a lot of fun**

21. Productivity Journal - Either goal-setting forward momentum (what you wish to achieve) or tracking what you have already achieved or both. When we make time to record the 'to do' list we have already completed we become more aware of what we have completed

22. Limiting Beliefs or Positive Beliefs Journaling

23. Past - Present - Future Journaling (changing perspectives) looking back positively, reflecting now on the positives in the situation, forecasting a positive future

24. Recognition Journal (who made a difference to you today?) write about the people in your life who made your day a great day

25. Letter writing – These kinds of letters you generally don't send. It's a unique way of writing to the people you have encountered in your life who may have caused you pain. You get to choose how you'd like to write; these could also be gratitude letters to people who have influenced your life positively

26. **Notes to the Self – Writing the notes to yourself to include the words you never heard from the significant people in your life**

27. **Thank You Journaling – Open Communications Journal thanking your family/ group/spouse/team to acknowledge what you love and appreciate them for**

28. **Personal Poem Journal – Record your poetry, quotes and ditties from the heart**

29. **Self-love Journal - An expressive praise journal for recording what you like, love, respect and enjoy about who you are. You can include your unique gifts, skills, talents, abilities, etc.**

30. **Confidence & Self-esteem Journal – Write about the things you have achieved, your accomplishments and awards. You can also record this in the future tense writing about the future you who is going about his or her day confidently**

31. **Timeline Journaling - Recording your ancestry, childhood, past lives or future life expectation, future life creation**

32. **Daily, Weekly, Monthly Round-Up Journaling - Writing at the end of each day, week and month and year what you've learnt about yourself, others and your experiences**

33. Seasons Journaling - Write about the beginning, middle or end of each season and what you notice about the change of seasons and the passing of time

34. End of Year, Mid-Year, New Year or Monthly Reflection Journaling. There is no specific way to do this you can choose any of the exercises here and combine how you record these types of entries

35. Kindness Journaling - Recording kind words about yourself, the planet, friends, strangers, family etc. Writing about acts of kindness which you have witnessed or received is always heart-warming. You may like to leave kind words on pieces of paper and pin and leave them in random places

36. Happiness and Positivity Journal - What were the highlights of your day, week, month, year?

37. Prayer Journal – Write out prayer requests and give thanks for prayers already answered

38. Advice Journaling – 'Turning Problems to Solutions.' Writing to yourself from the standpoint of a wise guide, a spiritual guru, someone you admire, like and trust or advice from your future self who has moved beyond the current problem.

Detail the information they will they advise you when you think of a specific question, situation, worry or concern etc

39. Memories Journal - For this option, it is best if you write about happy memories when journaling. For painful and deeply traumatic memories, you may benefit from having a therapist, coach, emotional or mental health support practitioner to guide you for the duration or after completion of this programme.

40. Life Challenges Journal - Recording problems you have overcome or may currently be experiencing and what you've learnt about your strength, courage, resilience, personality, unique gifts and talents etc

41. Life Milestones Journaling - Detailing significant Birthdays, Anniversaries, Weddings, adversities and Celebrations etc

42. Energy Diary - Measuring when you are at peak state energetically and writing about it. Detail what time of the day do you feel at your best, what you were doing, how it makes you feel when energised? As writers, producing quality content is always best written when you are highly energised and at peak energy flow

43. **Mementoes Diary – Expressive writing about unique treasures you have, family heirlooms you plan to pass on or items found which are sentimental to you**

44. **Poetry and Quotes - Read a quote or poem a day and write about it or make up your own**

45. **Relationship Journaling - Record your thoughts, feelings and emotions in your journal. Detail what you may be holding back from saying or doing what you would like to for whatever reason. You may also want to record what you love, appreciate and enjoy about your relationships (family/ significant other, friendship, working relationships etc. are all valid here)**

46. **Feelings Journal - Write down feelings as they come up, i.e. Sadness, Anger, Fear, Happiness, Joy, Excitement etc. Notice the location of where you feel these feelings in your physical body and how they present (i.e. heat, rushing sensation, coolness, pain, tension etc.)**

47. **Power Writing Journal (used to raise your energy) - Write a story, snippet or poem which makes you feel excited, motivated, energised and alive, build the momentum and feeling of positive expression as you write**

48. **Creative Writing Journal - A storytelling journal of actual or fictitious happenings**

49. **Character Development Journaling - Detailing characters you meet on the bus, at the supermarket, friends of friends etc. You may like to use the characters if writing a fiction book**

50. **'The End' Journaling - Whatever it is that's stopping you from moving forwards in your life, write about 'The End.' Say goodbye to the part of you who was holding onto this story. Once written, you can rip your paper into confetti, burn it, throw darts at it or put it in the rubbish bin or some other 'method' to close that chapter of your life and move forward.**

51. **Inner-child Stories Journal - Stories to heal. What stories would your younger self love to have heard, written about, or been part of an enriching experience? Write an account with your younger self as the main character (it can be a real or fictional story or both)**

52. **Stress Release Journaling - Write out your stressors.**

53. **Anxiety and Worry Journal - Write down your worries and be sure to seek professional therapeutic support in addition to journaling if things become emotionally overwhelming for you**

54. **Dream Journal - Write about your dreams and what they mean to you**

55. **Magic Moments Journaling - Write about a past magical moment or the special moment you would like to create for yourself or others in the future**

56. **Most Amazing Memories Journal - Detail if full sensory experience the most amazing, extraordinary, precious experiences and memories you have enjoyed. What did you see, hear, feel, smell and taste? What was the predominant sense in this memory? What is the mood and emotion you remember the most?**

57. **Limitless Journaling - Write about (in present tense) 'acting as if' you are on holiday or living in the country of your ideal destination, journal 'as if' your dreams have come true, express your passions fully ignited and fulfilled.**

58. **Mantras and Affirmations Journal - Record positive words, thoughts, vibrations and intentions in your journal**

59. **Travel, Vacation and Holiday Journal - Record your travels and adventures as you go along. You may like to detail and map the holidays and weekends away you have experienced so far and make a list where you'd like to visit in the future**

60. **Nature Journal - Visit new places, hug a tree, watch a bumblebee or butterfly gathering pollen and write about what you experienced inwardly. If you can't get outside, look at stimulating nature photographs or videos. Write about your sensory experiences in the presence of nature. How did it feel, what did you see, smell, hear, taste and sense? Record what you notice about life and the natural environment descriptively, season, month, time of day, time temperature, weather, visual details, smells, tastes, textures, sounds and your experience of what you encountered**

61. **Food Journal (what did you taste, what nourished you, quenched your thirst, what flavours did you enjoy?)**

62. **Exercise and activity Journal (what form of exercise energised motivated and inspired you)**

63. People Journal - What did you notice about co-workers, strangers, family, friends and your reaction to them? Writing about people in detail including their behaviours and quirks is an excellent tool for character development if writing fiction

64. Narrative Journaling - Either writing about your own stories for healing or the healing of others through storytelling

65. Questions and Answers Journaling. Use two different colour pens. One colour where you record the problem and two a different colour pen where you write in the solution. You write freely from both perspectives to discover and uncover the answer which was missing by trying to resolve a problem through thought alone

66. Environment - What impacted you negatively and positively about your circumstance and situation today? (home, workspace, means of travel, neighbourhood, community etc.)

67. Thank you - I love you Journal - Positive Journal to the Self (acknowledging your body, health, abilities, strengths, in acknowledgement of who you are and your amazing body with love, acceptance and approval)

68. **Positive Journaling for Others. Complete as above acknowledging your loved ones and the people who have made a difference to you**

69. **Future Self Journaling – writing from your future perspective looking back to now**

70. **Timed Journaling – set a timer for as long as you wish. Write as much as you can during this time.**

PART FOUR

SAYING YES TO YOU

WHEN ARE YOU BEING NICE AND WHEN ARE YOU BEING REAL?

Time waits for no man or woman come to that. Time is of the essence, get out of your way, set boundaries, say yes to making time for you and write from your heart. Your journal is waiting - Wendy Fry

What's the best that can happen when you write and speak from your heart?

Invitation

On researching why people don't write, stop writing or give up on the dream of writing and self-publishing their first book, it became evident to me the emotional side of needs attention. Writing isn't just about writing; it's about showing up as who you are. Confidently sharing your message. Writing and speaking from your heart. It's about gaining courage, sharing your truth and growing into YOU.

Until one is committed, there is hesitancy, the chance to draw back, always ineffectiveness, Concerning all acts of initiative (and creation), there is one elementary truth, the ignorance of which kills countless ideas and splendid plans: that the moment one definitely commits oneself, then Providence moves too. All sorts of things occur to help one that would never otherwise have occurred, A whole stream of events issues from the decision, raising in one's favour all manner of unseen incidents and meetings and material assistance, which no man could have dreamt would have come his way. I have learned a deep respect for one of Goethe's couplets:

Whatever you can do, or dream, begin it.

Boldness has genius, power and magic in it! - William Hutchinson Murray

BOUNDARIES

The act of putting pen to paper encourages pause for thought, this is turn makes us think more deeply about life, which helps us regulate our equilibrium - Norbet Platt

As a writing coach, I find many of my clients complain about not having enough personal space, writing time and privacy or metaphorically speaking they are juggling too many balls while riding the emotional rollercoaster of the writer's life. Whether it's walking the dogs, cooking the cat – oh, no I mean grooming the cat, children to feed, clothes to wash, shopping to buy and gardens to dig and that's before the working day begins! It's all too much.

You may be scratching your head or your armpit and if you've lost the plot scratching someone else's while wondering 'what can I DO about all the balls I'm juggling.'

Few people have mind-reading skills and whether it's your spouse, your boss, co-workers, friends, the bus driver while you are running your little legs off to catch the bus, the people in the line-up at the supermarket checkout being obnoxious or whoever it is you want to 'just get it and KNOW what you want.' I suggest you don't hold your breath waiting for IT to happen.

I need to have a quiet word in your ear - Complaining won't change it!

So, without further ado - Get on your feet – You can make it happen!

If something isn't working, this will help you get clear in expressing the voice of your heart and will support, you in starting your boundaries.

For writing to flow, you must make time to write!

GET ON YOUR FEET YOU CAN MAKE IT HAPPEN

This fabulous writing invitation (the title inspired by one of my music hero's Gloria Estefan)

When you focus on the goal at hand to carve out personal space and time for you, you can make a stand and get down to the business of writing. You can use this exercise on anything you wish.

Healthy Boundaries Writing Invitation

Find two sheets of A4 paper or equivalent

Draw a circle in the middle of each piece of paper with some space around it.

In the centre of one sheet write **'This is okay for me.'**

On the outside **'This isn't okay for me.'**

On the next sheet in the centre **'I AM'** and on the outside **'I AM NOT.'**

Complete both sheets.

Write down the inner and outer segments the statements of what is okay and what's not okay. I am this/I am not this.

To create healthy boundaries, you have to know what you don't want, communicate what you do want and follow up with re-setting those boundaries if people need a gentle reminder.

Complete this activity to define your boundaries and write from your heart.

When you are clear about what you want and set the example using clear, assertive communication, your boundaries are respected as you respect yourself. You may encourage others to be true to themselves – I invite you to be honest, dare to be you and share your unique voice.

MAKING TIME TO JOURNAL

"Don't die with your words inside you – set them free and live your life on purpose!" Wendy Fry

There are many benefits gained when writing daily for at least twenty minutes. You may be curious to set up research and journaling groups using my book as a foundation and record the benefits of both private and group journaling.

There are eighty-six thousand, four hundred seconds in a day. Time can't be banked, traded or saved for a rainy day. We get one shot at this life unless you believe in the afterlife. So, you may as well join me and make your days count.

There are various case studies and research statistics about the benefits of writing daily for at least twenty minutes. I'm not going to write a lengthy piece here because quite frankly it would be an attempt to stuff the page full of words and I'd just be filling time and wasting yours and mine. Time is a precious commodity, especially as a writer.

Let's keep it simple, and you will have more time to write. Begin with 10-15mins writing by hand and extend to more extended periods as and when the mood hits.

REASONS OR EXCUSES?

Seventy-six excuses are not reason enough not to write. You've been lying to yourself. If you want to write, you WILL find the way!

Invitation

Write out the following list ideally on one piece of paper

1. Getting started
2. Confidence
3. yourself
4. Patience
5. Distractions
6. Pen or pencil running out
7. Guts
8. Writer's block
9. Laziness
10. Literacy

11. Finding your authentic voice
12. Self-judgement
13. Perception of another person's judgement
14. Need for validation or approval
15. Time management
16. Self-prioritising
17. Overwhelm
18. Work
19. Homelife
20. Emotions
21. Procrastination
22. Taking responsibility
23. Life Events
24. Self-sabotage
25. Fear of failure
26. Shame
27. Guilt
28. Embarrassment
29. Vulnerability
30. Memory

31. Lack of ideas
32. Too many choices
33. Environmental triggers
34. Finances
35. Being seen
36. Perceived criticism
37. Self-criticism
38. Negative self-beliefs
39. Self-doubt
40. Negative opinions from others
41. Articulation
42. Forgetfulness
43. Energy
44. Motivation
45. Lack of focus
46. Exposure
47. Fear
48. Perceived rejection or criticism
49. Comparison
50. Honing your creative process

51. Not feeling/believing 'you're good enough.'
52. Self-esteem
53. Confidence
54. Physical disability
55. Learning Label (Dyslexia etc.)
56. Intimidation
57. Depression
58. Stagnation
59. Self-discipline
60. Perfectionism
61. Boredom
62. Emotions, thoughts and feelings
63. Writer's block
64. Self-acceptance
65. Hopelessness
66. Learning about how to write
67. Lack of self-belief
68. Having your written works accepted
69. Having your written works rejected
70. Illness

71. Developing positive writing habits
72. Not completing what you've started
73. Your inner critic
74. Self-judgement
75. Completing things
76. Finding your writing community
77. Other reason or excuse – Please add to your list

Well done. Now, tear it up and turn it into a confetti storm.

Shout out loud and proud, ''I'm done with that!''

Seventy-six excuses are not reason enough not to write. You've been lying to yourself. If you want to write, you WILL find the way!

Now write this down

I am a fantastic writer

Pat yourself on the back for making time for you!

Clap your hands together and shout ''hoorah.''

Point to yourself and say, ''I AM a Writer!''

Cartwheels, high fives Goddess and Warrior dances and another extravaganza optional.

And now we have calmed down.

Let's get down the business of writing!

ITS TIME TO STOP WASTING TIME

Use the following exercise to fully understand how much time you have to share your message, passion and purpose.

Invitation

1. Fold in 4 equal portions vertically (in half and half again)
2. Along the bottom write the numbers 0 –120 as 30, 60, 90, along with the three folds 0 and 120 at either end
3. Mark off the age you are now on the timeline
4. Mark off the age you think you will live to
5. Rip off the past (the numbers before the age you are now) The past is over.
6. Tear off the future.
7. What if you're right about the number of years you have left to write and self-publish your book?
8. What is the exact number of years you have left?

9. What thoughts come to mind when you realise your perceived longevity?
10. What feelings are present?
11. Does this realisation scare you or motivate you?
12. How can you most effectively use your remaining time?
13. What actions can you take to prioritise writing your book?

WRITING TOPIC IDEAS

The opportunities to write are endless. Here are just a few writing ideas relating to the concept of time. Further into Write from Your Heart, you will find many invitations, including 365 Days of journaling topic prompts.

- ✓ You've woken up in a different time where you have all the time you want to write from your heart. Where are you, what do you see, hear, smell, taste and sense, what does it feel like being here? What else would you like to add to this 'space.'
- ✓ What do you love most about being in this time and space? - write about your experience in your journal
- ✓ How do you fill your time and make it work for you?

Heart-Centred Wisdom Writing Exercise

Wherever you go, go with all your heart – Confucius

Use the following process to connect deeply with your heart centre to encourage the flow of journal writing. You can pose any questions to the next exercise as you wish to gain intuitive knowing to support you with your life choices.

1. Take your mind to the location of your heart. Focus on your heart centre (the area of your heart chakra indicated at the site of palms meeting in front of the chest and heart space in this diagram)

2. Place your hands if you wish to instead of palm to palm, directly over the centre of your chest laying one hand flat on top of the other and take deep breaths in and out.

3. Become aware of the warmth of your hands as they rest together over your heart centre.

4. The connection made helps to stabilise your heart and connect you with your heart's innate intelligence and information centre.

5. Slow down your breathing, taking your breath down to your stomach area. When breathing in this way and slowing down your breathing, you stimulate the relaxation response. A deeper breath can be noted by your stomach, which will expand on breathing in and on breathing out decrease the distension. Breathing this way has many health as well as emotional benefits.

6. Build a sense of gratitude, caring, compassion and love as you focus on the love in your life, your blessings and joys. Feel the love in your heart growing as your heart centre expands when you focus on the abundance in your life and your experiences.

7. Ask your heart a silent, straightforward question, e.g. *''What do I need to know about this choice, opportunity or person, etc.? ''*

8. When connecting with your heart, you may experience a sense of calmness, peace, expansion and stillness. You may notice too warm, cold or tingling sensations as energy moves around your energy body which may also seem like the physical body. If you do not experience such changes, this is okay too, we each experience this exercise differently and it may take a little time to get used to a new way of breathing and being. Stay with this exercise until you find yourself moving

away from trying to think of the answer with your rational mind and ask the heart again what it is you need to know.

9. This sequence takes you on an inner journey where you can leave the outside world for a short space of time and gain deeper emotional understanding and focus

10. Answers may come into your awareness as 'spoken words' in the form of mental messages or as sensations in the body. Use your breath and heart centred focus until the answer comes to you.

11. Daily heart centred focus and breathing will support in many ways with your writing process. It's a fabulous way to get out of 'overthinking' and to enjoy being in the moment with this practice.

TURNING PROBLEMS TO SOLUTIONS

NOW is the time to let go of fear and indecision. It's time to ditch the limiting beliefs and outdated behaviours holding you back from being all you can be. Your past is not your future. Being aware of the past is helpful. Living there isn't. Say YES to sharing your message. Say yes YOU. Voice the truth of the author within.

You are not your story. You are not what happened to you, and you choose who you become.

1. Bring your current, and future projected challenge or problem to mind

2. Focus on your heart chakra indicated at the location of palms meeting in front of the chest. Place your hands if you wish to instead of palm to palm, directly over the centre of your chest fingers extending to your heart laying one hand flat on top of the other and take deep breaths in and out

3. Slow down your breathing, taking deep and easy breaths down to your stomach area. When breathing in this way and slowing down your breathing, you stimulate the relaxation response. A deeper breath can be noted by your stomach, which will expand on breathing in and on breathing out decrease the distension. Breathing this way has many health as well as emotional benefits.

4. Bring the problem you wish to find a solution to the front of your mind.

5. Next, imagine the problem moving across the top of your head and away from you.

6. Then take both your heart-centred awareness and the front of your mind to the perfect place in time and space where this problem no longer exists.

7. What do you notice?

8. Where are you?

9. What is the event or occasion?

10. Are you alone or with others?

11. What is the time of day, the year?

12. What do you see, hear, feel, smell, taste and sense?

13. Turn those feelings up, make the picture brighter stronger, clear, turn up the sounds, smells and tastes take some lovely deep breaths in and out.

14. Allow the sensory energy experience and to rise within you.

15. Send the new information out from your heart and into the direction of your future

16. Repeat as and when needed.

You get to choose how you think and feel at any given moment. Becoming energy and thought aware with your heart and mind connected, creates for ourselves, excellent opportunities.

There are many processes I use in work in supporting aspiring authors to write from their hearts. I use a variety of techniques to gain the information stored within to support in tapping into the data stream of energy. Some may call this The Universe, Source, Matrix, Field or some other such term.

I believe we all have the same infinite potential. It's often the ability to move metaphorically beyond the current thought limitations which enable us to create a new outcome.

FUTURE LIFE PROGRESSION – FUTURE VISION YOUR AUTHOR'S LIFE

Future Life Progression is a process developed by Anne Jirsch, one of the world's leading experts in Future Visioning.

As one of her worldwide FLP practitioners, Wendy offers FLP sessions online. www.wendyfry.com

Future Vision Your Author Life

Imagine how looking one, five, ten or more years into your future. How could it benefit you now? What could you change with the wisdom gained from peeking ahead?

Future Life Progression is a unique and safe way to look ahead into your future to find out what next steps to take in your life, now. It's a positive experience which can only change your life for the better.

What would it be like to learn how to overcome the personal and professional challenges you have right now?

What if you knew that making an individual choice was the right choice?

If you could gain insider information to find out if a specific job or relationship was right for you, would you?

If you are uncertain about a house move being the right move for you who will this benefit you long term?

What about finances. What if you intuitively knew when is the best time to invest?

Future Life Progression, sometimes known as future visioning, will give you all these answers and more. It's profoundly enriching to explore this journey at the start of writing your first book. You can find out title ideas, the best date to launch your book, book series ideas as well as who are the best people to support you in sharing your author voice.

If you could give your younger self some guidance after all the challenges, you have overcome what would you say? FLP is no different from that. The snapshots we gain in the future are the action steps we can take in the now.

Lara's Testimonial

I have a keen interest in Past Life Regression and knew very little about Future Life Progression. Although uncertain about travelling forward in time, I knew I needed to make crucial decisions in my life. I am setting up a business based on my first book.

My focus for the session was to see how my business would progress and how could I use my book in the way I imagined furthering my career.

I found the insight I gained from this session quite invaluable, as were the ideas regarding the direction my business would take. This session has helped me to streamline my thoughts and focus on one path. Looking back, it is now apparent what I should have been doing, but, in my confusion, I couldn't see it. I would recommend this to anyone who is looking for some direction in life. The session was relaxing, and I felt quite energised afterwards.

Gills Testimonial

Thank you so much for yesterday. I enjoyed the whole thing and got a lot out of it. I was feeling stuck and fearful of the future until you took me on the Future Life Progression Journey. I now feel a lot more motivated to get stuff done. You're really skilled and have a lovely way about you.

Deb's Testimonial

A few weeks on from our writing retreat, I feel like a different person. My heart is opening as I write. Wendy gives herself fully. She loves what she does. She is highly skilled and has an array of techniques and resources to help in any situation; you feel safe and held when working with her. FLP surprised me and has jumpstarted me into taking action and start writing down my book ideas.

YOUR YEAR AHEAD AS A WRITER

Imagine you have found your best way forward as a writer and author. You have found the next year to be the most successful it can be after applying the journaling techniques shared in Write from Your Heart.

Consider how much knowledge you have gained through journaling and discovering your author voice.

Open your mind and consider what's the best that can happen when you expand your writing life?

Recognise you have the potential to tap into the infinite stream of wisdom, abundance and talent in the world. All the information you need is there for you; all you need to do is to let it flow through you.

Think about what you have changed, what actions have you taken and what choices have you made to have your most successful year as a writer and one where you have made the most of your writing talents and opportunities.

What projects have you completed?

What new materials have you developed?

What are you planning?

What did you achieve in this past year to make the most of your talents?

What new belief have you formed about yourself and your ability to write?

What actions have you taken which have supported you to achieve your full potential?

What has been your greatest writing achievements?

What is the significant change in your work?

What new opportunities have come your way?

How did you make the most of the opportunities?

What is different about you?

What is your focus?

What are you writing?

Ask your future self what you need to know right now.

Make notes in your journal regarding your experience.

What have you stopped doing?

What have you started doing?

What are you doing differently?

Write a twelve-month plan of the monthly actions you will take to support you in reaching your goal.

What's the first action you can take now?

What additional actions can you take across the next fifty-two weeks of the year ahead?

How will taking these weekly and monthly actions in a specific time frame benefit your writing life?

If you'd like to be guided through this exercise book your 'Year Ahead as a Writer and Author' support session at www.wendyfry.com

Future Life Progression sessions are available across a range of topics online for your convenience.

Why wait when the future is in your hands. Contact Wendy to book your Future Life Progression session and use this technique in any area of your life. www.wendyfry.com

The future belongs to those who believe in the beauty of their dreams - Eleanor Roosevelt

PART FIVE

YOUR AUTHOR VOICE

YOUR AUTHOR VOICE

Her stories grew and changed as she tested them... but all of them started from a core of what she knew and sensed about people. And it was not even that she made up anything rather that she listened to herself - Ursula Hegi

Here are some topic ideas which make for insightful journaling pieces. You can write from several different perspectives in the first, second or third person. You can also explore characterisation as if you were developing a character from your own experiences.

Invitation

Who are you in your darkest hour?

How do your inner and outer behaviours change according to your mood?

What have you never told a soul?

What keeps you awake at night?

What or who do you love?

What ignites your passion?

Who or what do you stand for?

Who would you protect?

What joys do you wish to express?

What are your greatest successes?

What message do you want to share from your heart to inspire others?

In his book, The Four Agreements, Don Miguel Ruiz writes – *''our biggest fear is taking the risk to express want we really are."* Write from Your Heart is an opportunity to do just that.

OPEN, HONEST, AUTHENTIC COMMUNICATION

Authentic communication with your journal is the one place you can speak freely, underscored and let rip or indeed share your highs, goals, your dreams and in-betweens.

When it comes to communicating with authenticity, I will share openly with you. In the past, I, too, have held my voice back from speaking up for fear of upsetting others. The pain I felt physically inside from suppressing emotions became unbearable. In writing in my journal, I eventually found a way to heal past hurts. Feelings are always best expressed.

When we speak our truth and lift the mask, the presence of the writer's heart within has an opportunity to convey who we truly are. Your journal awaits, with a listening ear.

Your voice is your direct expression of you. Your unique message comes through your voice and you will carry it through the journaling process.

TIPS FOR DEVELOPING YOUR AUTHOR VOICE

- Release your inner voice freely in your journal
- Be 100% the real you, always
- Write for your enjoyment no one else's
- Stop apologising for being you
- Speak from your experience
- Record the facts or at least how you remember them
- Be authentic in your writing
- Share your story the way you remember it
- Stay consistent and write daily
- Get to know yourself through journaling
- Be expressive in your language
- Take responsibility to share your truth
- Share details about you, your thoughts, feelings and emotions
- Record your regrets, hopes, fears, joys, achievements and celebrations
- Allow the essence of 'you' to permeate your words

- Be the authority in your life and share your voice
- Express your concerns, needs, views and opinions
- Empower yourself and speak from your heart
- Find your unique voice through journaling

POSITIVE WRITING AFFIRMATIONS

Copy and write out the following statements in your journal and create your positive affirmation to inspire you to write daily.

The Power of "I am" Writing Exercise

Invitation

I am a writer

I am an author

I am a creative writer

I am an excellent writer

I am a published author

I am a best-selling author

I am a constant writer

I am a prolific writer

I am an author who writes great content

Every day in every way I am getting better and better

Please do add to the list with your affirmations and positive statements.

WRITER'S FLOW

You will have a story in there or a character, a place, a poem, a moment in time. When you find it, you will write it. Word after word after word - Patricia MacLachlan

Mission Statements for Writers

Copy and write out the following statements in your journal, adding to the account what you are inspired to write.

I love knowing my writing -

I love how it feels when my book -

I choose to journal every day because -

Writing every day helps me -

I am excited to write as it -

Writing from my heart enables me to -

I'm thrilled at the thought -

I love seeing myself –

You may wish to add to the prompts and extend your writing practice to beyond a paragraph of writing.

THE SPOTLIGHT PROCESS

Bring balance to your thoughts about writing.

I developed The Spotlight Process to help you acknowledge where you may have been spending most of your thought time and to guide you to achieve a better balance in your life and your writing habits.

If your thoughts were a laser beam lighting the way, where have you been shining your light? Past, Present or future? Is this working for you? If it's a big fat NO, something needs to change. Write about the changes and actions you will take to create a better future for yourself.

The steps below provide an opportunity to understand your thought process and what gets in the way of writing and sharing your author voice.

Where have you been shining your spotlight?

- **How often do you find yourself stuck in the past thinking the reasons not to start or complete your book?**
- **How much time do you spend thinking about your current problems and feel overwhelmed as a result?**
- **When do you find yourself negatively predicting the future of your ability to write and complete your book or book series?**

Now is the perfect time to apply The Spotlight Process by merely examining your thoughts.

- **Wherever you are at this moment, I invite you to think about a spotlight and the light which shines from it. Whether you see it, sense it or imagine it, think about that spotlight right now. This ray of light could be in the form of a torch, a lighthouse, a stage spotlight. Whatever spotlight comes to mind is perfect for you.**
- **Think of this ray of light as a ray of your thoughts, feelings and emotions. This light can shine back into your past, ahead to your future or into this very moment.**
- **You are in control of shining the light. You are the director of where you narrow your beam and where you place your focus.**

Whatever you shine your light on, you will experience.

- **Using The Spotlight Process, consider where you have been spending most of your thought time?**
- **Past, Present or Future?**
- **Examine your thoughts and feelings about the past. Are they positive or negative?**
- **How do you feel about your current circumstances NOW after using journaling to release aspects of your past stopping you from achieving what you wish to?**

THE SPOTLIGHT PROCESS – KEY QUESTIONS

I suggest you copy out these questions into your journal and refer to until they become a natural part of your thought process. Always use these questions if you're feeling in a low or negative mood before, during or after writing.

1. **Where is my thinking right now? (Past, Present or Future?)**
2. **What proportion of my thinking is negative?**
3. **How does it affect me and my writing when I focus on the negative?**
4. **Where is the evidence that what I think will happen will come to pass?**
5. **What do I want instead of thinking or feeling this way?**
6. **Coming from my heart instead of my head, what do I need to express in my journal?**

When you are clear about where you have been spending your thought time and how this may be limiting you and your writing ability, the path ahead is brighter and more achievable.

Using this process will support you as you bring your thoughts into balance and improve writing flow

Need some help to further your personal, professional or writing progress? There are options for both therapeutic emotional support and professional coaching and mentoring for aspiring authors.

Most new authors benefit from emotional catharsis before starting work together on a writing project to be sure you're in the best place to write. You'd be surprised how easy it is when you use the right techniques to move forward. I can help you do this with ease.

I welcome you to reach out and contact me at www.wendyfry.com to discuss the best support means of support to meet all your personal aims and writing needs.

THE *'WRITE'* TO SPEAK UP - This is not a typo

Autobiographic story is not just an account of events; it is the charting of your emotional, moral and psychological course, which gives meaning to those events - Tristine Rainer

Invitation

There will have been times in your life when you never felt heard. Perhaps times, when you did attempt to speak up you, were silenced.

If You have experienced too much squashing of your expression in the past, your author voice will need encouragement to speak up.

Now is the to write your story of silence in whichever way feels right for you.

Write about the following situations in your journal.

- ✓ When in your experience were expectations put upon you to do things the 'right' way?
- ✓ What was that like for you?
- ✓ Did you go with the flow or rebel?

- ✓ When were you told you had no right to do, be or have something which was important to you?
- ✓ How often have you felt like you've done the wrong thing even if you were trying to do the right thing with the knowledge, learning and wisdom you had at the time?

When we fear to get something wrong, we play small and often act passively. We tend not to speak up, keeping our thoughts and feelings locked away inside. Journaling is the perfect place to speak freely and let your words flow as you write. Your journal is listening. Extend any of the exercises as you read through Write from Your Heart. You may even like to write up a list of questions to share in a book club and writing group and further your discussion of each exercise shared.

CIRCLE OF LIFE

Are you self-sabotaging as an aspiring author and telling yourself you don't have what it takes? Enough I say. It's time to stop that story and begin a new one. Write a different future into being - Wendy Fry

As a qualified therapist, in my hypnosis sessions working with my writing coaching clients, I invite the person I am working with to imagine they are walking along a beach. The creative journey takes them to find the perfect open space, and they draw a large circle around themselves in the sand.

Within the circle, they write down representations of emotional pain and any limiting beliefs they may have about their ability to write and the fear of other people's judgement. They record all their hurts, unkind words heard or spoken, past and future worries, overwhelming feelings etc. are recorded in the sand.

Symbols, pictures, initials of people, names, words, initials relating to a person who has caused them pain are all marked in the sand. Shells, driftwood and pebbles etc. are placed into the circle to form additional representations of the thoughts, feelings and emotions which are holding the client back from writing and completing their book etc.

They then step out of the circle and watch as the tide comes in as it washes away all the hurts and pains of the past along with future based doubts and fears.

They then create a new circle in the sand further back from the water's edge and add to it the desired outcomes for the future, sending these positive intentions to the source to be manifested.

You may wish to re-create this exercise and adapt it as a drawing and writing opportunity in your journal or by some other means.

The Circle of Life hypnosis coaching session is a deeply relaxing way of working with me to move on from the past, making your future a happier place to be. Find out more about hypnosis for authors here. www.wendyfry.com

I AM 'SOMEBODY.'

I have used this process with teenagers and adults in workshops to understand the words we hold inside, which may continue to hurt us if left unaddressed.

We stick together sheets of wallpaper or flipchart paper big enough for the person to stand in front of pinned to a wall or to simply lay the paper down and the person whose turn it is laying down on top of the paper.

The groups work together to draw around each other's bodies, and inside the imprint of their shape, they write all the unkind names they've heard, the negative beliefs held about themselves or what they believe others hold about them. They write down the words people have yelled at them in anger or disagreement, judgement etc. All limiting beliefs, past hurts and future doubts and fears go into the body outline.

Any 'body shames' physical injuries, emotional injuries, mental scars etc. can be marked in colour or a symbol, dot, to indicate ''this is what I am walking around with.'' We stick it up on the wall ''all bodies together.''

We look, we see what we don't want to see or hold onto anymore – it's too much to continue to carry these stories around.

Next, we take a clean sheet, a new page we create a new outline.

Each person writes on the page, positive words of affirmation. They write about their skills, unique gifts, personal attributes and amazing talents. The person in question writes on new positive, inspiring beliefs and statements about what they can be, do or have. They add meaning to their life and 'embody' it all.

Smaller body outlines on A4 paper or cardboard cut-outs of a male or female shape can also be purchased or created to simplify this exercise.

I must tell you how moving this exercise is to facilitate and to watch. It comes from my experience of working in schools in 'Behaviour Support' as an ELSA (Emotional Literacy Support Assistant) and the group support work I offered within the school setting.

I know for fact words change lives. They may lift us up or tear us down and become the inner dialogue of our lives if left unaddressed. What can you say to another to heal hurts and invite them to be somebody?

REFLECTIONS FOR PERSONAL GROWTH

"I had a very dysfunctional family, and a very bad childhood so I made a world out of words. And it was my salvation." Mary Oliver

Notice the time of day when you read this. The month. The year. The season. Slow yourself right down and breathe.

Take a moment to reflect on the highs and lows of the past year what you learnt, what you moved through, the things you overcame, and what you achieved.

There are eighty-six thousand four hundred seconds in a day, to appreciate and enjoy. to begin again perhaps differently this time. You don't need to repeat the same mistakes you made last year. Your past need not define your future. Think of any difficulties you experienced as a learning curve. Take stock of what you need to stop doing, start doing or do differently in the year ahead to reach your highest potential.

Whatever goals you have whether in the area of health, personal relationships, career, personal development, family, finances or fun and recreation the intentions you set now with energised action and adhere to are more likely to come to fruition.

You can adapt this exercise if you wish to and use it as an 'end of day reflection,' 'month-end' or 'year-end' strategy to work out your next steps in life and to live it to your best advantage.

Personal Reflections Exercise

Take some time out to write up your reflections in your journal. You can complete the exercise in brief in one sitting or spread across one entry per day until you have completed the invitation.

Invitation

- ✓ **What happened month by month?**
- ✓ **What did you love most about the year?**
- ✓ **What made you smile?**
- ✓ **What were your magical and happy moments?**
- ✓ **What made you cry?**
- ✓ **What happened in the past year you would prefer not to go through again?**
- ✓ **What did you learn about yourself because of the year's events?**

- ✓ **What do you need to change in your life in terms of health, relationships, finances, family, personal development, spirituality, fun and free time, career, home environment, how you spend your time etc.?**
- ✓ **What lessons have you learnt about yourself, people in general, your body, your work, family, relationships and your sense of fulfilment and accomplishment?**
- ✓ **What do you want for the year ahead? (Answer in the positive sense)**
- ✓ **What are you committed to achieving for the year ahead? (break this down into monthly and weekly goals.**
- ✓ **What's an essential skill to develop or master within yourself?**
- ✓ **What changes are you committed to acting on in your life?**
- ✓ **What do you need to do in the year ahead to get to where you want to be?**
- ✓ **If the last year was a tough year for you, how can you use your learning from this experience to your best advantage and make next year even better?**

- ✓ **What can you achieve in the next twelve months, three years and five years with focused attention?**
- ✓ **Who were you when you started this year, and who are you now?**
- ✓ **Who are you becoming?**
- ✓ **What else is possible for you?**

For sure, there are many questions here and ones you will benefit from when you take the time to stop and reflect on the past. Use your experiences, challenges and setbacks to your highest good. Being aware of the past is helpful, living there isn't!

Focus on your future, plan, take action every day towards your goals and dreams. Learn from setbacks, celebrate achievements and always remember every day you get to choose how you show up, how you react and respond in any situation. The meanings and beliefs you place on experiences. The filter in which you look through at the world. Nothing is set in stone if something isn't working change it.

Turn your face to the future, and you cannot see the past. Begin now as you mean to go on. Today is the first day of the rest of your life!

365 DAYS OF JOURNALING TOPICS

Writers are special people. Every person is a special kind of writer - Elsa Gidlow

Use the following topic ideas to commit to writing every day of the year. If preferred to choose the questions which most appeal to you most and write about them in your journal. If my questions stimulate new ideas for you or you, wish to frame the question differently, adapt the item to suit yourself.

Invitation

1. When you last wrote by hand, what was it you wrote?
2. A genie has gifted you a wish to create the perfect space for writing, describe it.
3. Who or what do you love?
4. What do you enjoy doing for fun?
5. How did you make it this far despite those challenges you thought you'd never overcome?
6. What do you remember about learning to read and write?
7. What are the top three things you most like about yourself?

8. If you could change one thing about yourself, what would it be?
9. Who has been your most significant positive influence up to now?
10. What are your favourite words?
11. When did you last have a great conversation?
12. How has your life as a child impacted your life both positively and negatively as an adult?
13. Write about the blessings in your life
14. What's your favourite book genre to read?
15. What kind of books do you avoid reading?
16. Who or what broke your heart?
17. If you could live your past over again, what would you change?
18. What makes you angry and how does your anger impact you or others?
19. What emotion do you need to release, which may be holding you back from writing your first book?
20. Who or what do you miss the most in your life?
21. If you could relive one specific day of your life over again, what day would it be?
22. What physical, mental and emotional health challenges have you overcome?
23. How has your family life changed since childhood?

24. What was your favourite toy, game or activity as a child?
25. What's your favourite colour, and why do you love it so much?
26. What have been your most significant challenges when it comes to writing?
27. What do you love about writing?
28. When do you last remember learning a new word?
29. What fascinates you?
30. What obsesses you?
31. How well do you deal with change?
32. What is your life calling and purpose?
33. Who or what frustrates you?
34. What area of the creative arts stimulates you?
35. As a child who let you down or failed you?
36. If you had unlimited resources what global, medical or scientific problem would you wish to solve?
37. Who is or was your greatest love?
38. What smell and taste bring back happy memories for you?
39. Where were you emotionally a year, five years and ten years ago?
40. How do you want your life to be in a year, five years and ten years?

41. List three facts others may not know about you
42. What keeps you awake at night?
43. How often do you have in-depth discussions? What do you love or hate about going deep?
44. What themes keep reoccurring in your life, health, work, relationships? (both positive and negative)
45. Where in the world would you most like to travel?
46. Which subject did you enjoy most at school?
47. Write about your relationship with technology (phone, PC, devices)
48. If you were to write a regular blog, what subjects will you cover?
49. What is your greatest accomplishment?
50. What excites you about the year ahead?
51. Which spiritual beliefs support and guide you?
52. What were the 'missing events' in your life you wish you had experienced?
53. When have you risked your life to save someone?
54. How well do you get along with your siblings?
55. What are your best traits?
56. What are your worst traits?
57. What is your saddest memory?
58. How did you start doing something you love?

59. What has been the most fabulous year of your life?
60. When you relax, what do you do?
61. What are your lesser strengths?
62. What are your greater strengths?
63. When have you visited a museum what has been the most fantastic thing you have seen or learnt?
64. If a friend spoke to you in the same way, you talked to yourself, how long would you allow them to be your friend?
65. What is the most sensible thing you've heard anyone say?
66. How does uncertainty make you feel?
67. What do you love and hate about social media?
68. What rituals do you have which comfort you?
69. If you had a massive win on the lottery, what would you spend it on?
70. What belief do you hold with which few people agree?
71. How often have you felt disappointed with life?
72. What's your favourite memory?
73. When you think about your family, what does it bring up for you?
74. What would you like to do more frequently?
75. How easy do you find it to ask for help?

76. What images, colours and styles are you drawn to for your home, fashion, workspace?
77. Who are your favourite actors, artists, musicians, composers, writers and poets?
78. What are your favourite songs, nursery rhymes and stories?
79. Write about a beautiful gift you have given or received
80. Who are your friends, and what do they have in common?
81. What relationships do you value the most?
82. What makes you angry, upset, up happy, afraid?
83. What brings you joy, happiness, love?
84. When was the last time you did something for the first time?
85. If you could change the world, what would you do?
86. When did you last celebrate something important to you?
87. What is the most memorable piece of writing you have read or written?
88. If you had a TV or radio show who would you like to interview and why?
89. What do you remember about your school years?

90. What place, city or country do you consider to be your home?
91. How have you processed grief when someone you love has left your life?
92. Who or what stirs your emotions, both positively and negatively?
93. What emotion do you wish you didn't feel?
94. Write about forgiveness, what are your beliefs around forgiving and being forgiven?
95. When you are feeling unhappy, what cheers you up?
96. What to do you stand for, what are your goals, values and ideals?
97. Who or what do you defend?
98. What would you create if you had funding?
99. What causes you to be anxious?
100. If you could be an animal, what would you be and why?
101. What's your best life experience so far?
102. Which season do you enjoy the most?
103. What makes you feel alive?
104. Write about which emotions motivate you positively
105. What family traditions do you have growing up?

106. How do you feel about Valentine's Day, Mother's Day, Father's Day, Christmas Day and other celebrated national days?
107. What's your preferred way to exercise?
108. What part of your life or your work would you like to outsource?
109. How well do you know yourself?
110. What have you recently learned about yourself which surprised you?
111. What leadership skills and qualities do you have?
112. How do you manage your time and is it time well spent?
113. What rules do you have for yourself and others?
114. How do you deal with perceived rejection, criticism and judgement?
115. What is the loveliest compliment you've ever received?
116. Write a thank you letter to someone who has touched your life positively
117. Write a letter to your past self and future self-telling them what you like, love and appreciate. Offer words of praise, thanks and encouragement
118. Write a letter to your fantastic body thanking all your body parts and functions for what they do for you. 'My Amazing Body'

119. 2,4,6,8 who do you appreciate. Write about the positive influencers in your life?
120. What is your favourite quote of all time?
121. What have you lost which you still miss?
122. How full is your glass?
123. If you were to 'get out of the box' where would you go
124. What did you want to be, do as a child? How closely are you living that ideal?
125. Who are the most important people in your life right now?
126. What makes you unique?
127. How much sleep are you getting? Is it enough or too much?
128. Thinking about your eating habits, what could you improve?
129. What would be your ideal working day?
130. Which kind of holiday do you prefer, Summer, Winter, relaxing or action orientated?
131. What is causing you stress in your life right now?
132. How do you overcome fear?
133. What skill could you teach in two minutes?
134. What has been your favourite New Year celebration to date?
135. Write about your ideal day when you're not working and taking time out?

136. What makes you worry?
137. When was the last time you asked for help?
138. What changes could you make to benefit your physical, emotional and spiritual health?
139. Name five things you could not live without and what it means to you to have them in your life
140. What does your 'work' mean to you?
141. How do you express yourself, creatively?
142. What would make you happy right now?
143. What habit would you like to break?
144. What habit would you welcome having, which positively serves you?
145. What has life taught you?
146. How do you deal with loneliness or boredom?
147. What makes you feel at peace?
148. When you encounter life's challenges and obstacles, how do you deal with them?
149. How do you want people to remember you when you are no longer on this earthly plane?
150. What makes you afraid?
151. What significant changes have you noticed in your life, neighbourhood, relationships, lifestyle health and finances in the ten years?
152. What'd the best advice you've received?
153. What are your personal and professional boundaries?

154. What are you saying yes to which doesn't serve you?
155. What do you know of your parent's lives before they met, and you came into the world?
156. How would a stranger describe you?
157. How would you describe yourself?
158. When are you at your most confident?
159. What do you love about life?
160. What'd the most embarrassing thing that has ever happened to you?
161. Who inspires you?
162. What has shocked you which you thought you'd never overcome?
163. Write about the last positive surprise you received
164. What life experiences, events and situations have made you feel ashamed, guilty or regretful?
165. When you feel nervous, uncertain or afraid, what words of encouragement can you give yourself to get back on track?
166. If you could describe your life in one word, what would it be?
167. What do you need in your life to feel safe?
168. Would you class yourself as an introvert or extravert?
169. How often do you feel overwhelmed?

170. How do you manage these feelings?
171. If you could change one thing about your childhood, what would it be?
172. What has changed your outlook on life?
173. Who do you admire who you would like to meet?
174. If there is someone from your past, you would like to meet again who would that be?
175. What kind of feedback do you welcome from others?
176. How do you currently relieve stress?
177. What hobbies and pastimes have remained current in your family?
178. Who has influenced your life positively?
179. When did you go the extra mile for someone with the goodness of your heart?
180. What manners are essential to you when being served by someone?
181. How often do you cry or speak to others about your problems?
182. What are your best childhood memories?
183. What have you resolved personally and professionally?
184. Thinking back to yourself as a child, what do you wish you'd known?
185. Who was your most significant influence growing up?

186. What helps you heal?
187. Who or what annoys you and why?
188. What's the best birthday party or celebration you've ever had?
189. What do you want to achieve in the area of your career?
190. What would you like to change in your neighbourhood?
191. Describe your ideal home. What does it look like, smell, like, feel like, what can you taste and sense from spending time there? Describe the décor, the furnishings, the land around.
192. Write about your most beloved pet
193. Describe your finances or 'lack of' and then write about them if they were a million times improved
194. What are your views on suicide, euthanasia, abortion, drugs, homelessness, mental health, domestic violence and other seemingly controversial subjects not always discussed freely
195. How has your experience of grief and loss impacted you?
196. What do you regret?
197. What toy did you want as a child which you never had?
198. Describe your last attempt to do something which although it was hard you eventually mastered

199. What motivates you to achieve your goals?
200. Write about a time you felt helpless. What did you do to get through this period?
201. What makes you happy?
202. How many items are on your bucket list, and what can you tick off next?
203. Who are you envious of and how does this impact you?
204. How would you describe your singing voice?
205. When it comes to dancing, are you a mover, shaker or wallflower?
206. What advice would you give to someone who has just started dating?
207. How would you best advise someone to get over a relationship breakup?
208. When has a teacher, mentor or coach inspired you, and what would you say to them now in recognition of their support?
209. When your mood is low, what do you think causes this?
210. What do you do to cheer yourself up?
211. What are the little things which make you happy?
212. What has been your funniest experience to date?
213. What subject or topic do you love learning?
214. When you look up at the sky, what do you notice?

215. Describe the most fantastic nature scene you have ever experienced?
216. Write about a season Spring, Summer, Autumn or Winter which is the most poignant for you
217. What's your favourite item in your wardrobe?
218. What fabrics do you like to wear?
219. Describe your wallet, purse or bag and contents within
220. What events have brought you closer to your family and friends?
221. Write about or draw a symbol or representation of your personality
222. What music do you dance to outrageously when no one is watching?
223. Are you a slow or fast eater? Do you taste your food, aware of what and how much you are eating?
224. What would you love to try out though may not for fear of another person's judgement or self-judgement?
225. What sports do you love which you play well?
226. Imagine you've arranged a blind date, what's the best that can happen?
227. Write about something you made which went badly wrong
228. Who has come to your rescue and 'saved the day' for you?

229. Describe a time when you won, achieved or excelled at something, what was that like for you?
230. How much self-control do you have?
231. What would you like to reveal about yourself to others you have yet to share?
232. Finish this statement - My best advice is -
233. Sunrise or sunset – which do you prefer and why?
234. Write about the journey your feet have taken you on, where have they been?
235. What makes your heart beat rapidly with excitement?
236. Write a love story – who are the main characters, and how does it end?
237. What are your superstitions?
238. Write about a time when you made up a name, pseudonym or had a specific nickname
239. Write about Algebra and your experience of it
240. Which health and wellbeing routines and tips do you a favour?
241. What are your family's stories of hardships, sacrifices and difficulties?
242. What relationship did you handle the end of badly?
243. Write about a time capsule you would like to create for yourself, what year, planet or dimension, where would you like to travel?

244. I believe in - finish the statement and the reasons why you believe
245. Rock stars are - finish the sentence and add as much detail as you wish
246. What was the most upsetting 'goodbye' you had to make?
247. What's been the favourite icebreaker activity?
248. What did you believe in as a child which you no longer buy into now, i.e. Tooth Fairy, Father Christmas?
249. When have you helped a stranger and expected nothing in return or been offered help out of the blue?
250. What superpowers do you wish you had?
251. What smells and tastes do you not enjoy?
252. What do you fear about the ageing process?
253. Describe the favourite landmarks you have visited
254. What is the 'magic' ingredient?
255. What have you and your family or friends accomplished together?
256. If you could be a force of nature, what would you be?
257. If you could hire unpaid helpers to support, you what would be their roles?
258. What constitutes a struggle for you emotionally, physically and mentally?

259. What are your opinions about children?
260. What are your thoughts about politics, and how does this impact you personally?
261. What words trigger you?
262. What would you never say in public, to someone's face though may say behind the other persons back?
263. How do you show or tell other people you love them?
264. When the bus, train, plane or taxi arrives on time, what do say or do?
265. When the bus, train, plane or taxi arrives late, what do you say or do?
266. When was the last time you donated to charity, a charity shop, homeless person or good cause? What did you give which made a difference to the receiver and you personally?
267. Write about the best music concert, show, event, festival, party or adventure you've ever been on
268. Who has seen your scars both the visible and invisible?
269. When thinking about death and dying, what comes up for you?
270. When you come across a brass band, steel band, merry-go-round or children's ride playing music or singing a song, what do you do?

271. What do you think makes a successful person successful?
272. Who from history inspires you?
273. What did you learn about money from your parents or the people who raised you?
274. What did you learn about relationships from your parents or people who raised you?
275. What did you learn at school which you now think was a waste of time?
276. What makes you laugh out loud?
277. What sounds irritate you?
278. Who is your favourite speaker, presenter or host?
279. What do you have in your possession which you said you would give back and haven't for whatever reason?
280. If someone offered to help you out what would you ask of them?
281. Who are you not speaking with or estranged from who you wish would communicate, make peace with you, apologise for etc.?
282. What makes you stamp your feet?
283. How do you feel about introducing different groups of friends with each other?
284. How good a friend, are you?
285. To dust or not to dust, that is the question? What do you love or hate about dusting?

286. What is your morning routine, and what could you add to it to make your day ahead more fun?
287. When you go to sleep at night what's generally the last thing on your mind?
288. What book or film has been pivotal in your life?
289. If you were to write a screenplay or life-changing book, what is the title?
290. If you got out of yourself out of your way, what will you be doing?
291. At the park what's your favourite ride or piece of equipment you still can't resist playing on as an adult?
292. If you had a metal detector, what treasure or object would you have liked to discover?
293. Are you decisive or indecisive person or can't decide? Write about that
294. What are your life priorities and values?
295. If someone is not respecting you, how do you let them know?
296. What's one thing you believe you can't give up?
297. What creative pursuits do you enjoy?
298. What do you believe would make the world a better place for all?
299. When you must focus on something important, how do you do this?

300. What's in your junk draw which needs chucking out?
301. What possessions no longer bring you joy?
302. What are you hoarding which you know intuitively is not suitable for you?
303. Fancy dress – love it or hate it? Why so?
304. Who is your hero?
305. What collaboration or shared venture are you currently enjoying?
306. What past venture was a huge success?
307. How much do you love yourself right now?
308. What do people love about you?
309. What did you witness in your past that you wish you hadn't?
310. If you could offer your 'future self' some words of wisdom, what would you say?
311. When you've stopped making excuses and procrastinating what will you start?
312. Write about the six people living or dead you would you like to invite to dinner?
313. What makes you want to run and hide?
314. When you purchased the last thing on impulse, what did you buy, do you regret it?
315. How do you express what makes you happy?
316. How often, are you kind, loving, generous and compassionate toward yourself?

317. What makes you feel free?
318. When did you break the rules and got found out?
319. How often do you reflect on your life and the short-term and long-term choices you're making?
320. What did you do when you overheard a conversation which you wish you hadn't?
321. What pranks, jokes and tricks have you fallen for or played on others?
322. Write about a time when 'enough was enough', and you chose to walk away?
323. What song holds special memories for you?
324. What makes you feel young?
325. Who would you like to cook dinner for you?
326. In which era do you wish you'd lived?
327. How do you deal with shock?
328. When did you apply for a job and felt relieved you weren't accepted?
329. Who do you wish you'd said hello to or asked out on a date?
330. When did you accept a job, role or position and wish you hadn't'?
331. What do you like and dislike about online relationships?
332. How would you like to spend your time in retirement?

333. If you could design an app, what will it include?
334. What will you work at relentlessly at until the job complete?
335. What was the most significant risk you ever took?
336. How do you feel right at this moment?
337. Chocolate, strawberry, vanilla or Cherry Garcia?
338. What can you do, say or change to feel more content and happier in your life?
339. What made you smile today, yesterday, this week, this month, this year?
340. What makes you nervous?
341. What are your favourite cartoons and animations? What do you love about them?
342. What societal 'rules' or conditions you've made up about men or women which you feel stay in place?
343. When have you chosen to quit something if it wasn't in alignment with your highest good?
344. What typo have you made which has got you in trouble or at least made other people laugh?
345. What objects do you own that tell a story about your life or how you see yourself?
346. What beliefs have your parents or caregivers handed down to you?
347. What have been your happiest memories from the year so far?

348. What's your happy ending?
349. What do you strive to achieve?
350. When character do you identify within your favourite book and why
351. What are your best tips for learning and studying?
352. What poem, story or song stands out for you?
353. What are you envisioning for your future?
354. How much are you focusing on 'acting as if' your goals had already come to pass?
355. What do you wish you'd dared to do?
356. What went into you achieving your most challenging goals?
357. I love knowing – Complete the sentence
358. I love how it feels when – Complete the sentencc
359. I've decided – Complete the sentence
360. More and more – Complete the sentence
361. It excites me – Complete the sentence
362. I love the idea – Complete the sentence
363. I'm excited at the thought – Complete the sentence
364. I love seeing myself – Complete the sentence
365. Eighty-six thousand seconds in a day. If today was your last day of the 'Precious Present' how will you choose to spend yours?

PART SIX

POWER WRITING

WRITING FROM YOUR HEART

Make your choice adventurous stranger. Strike the bell and bide the danger, or wonder, till it drives you mad, what would have followed if you had - The Magician's Nephew, C.S Lewis

My clients often ask me for writing tips and insider secrets and want to know how I got my first book written in six months (fifty-five thousand words). My second in nine months (eighty-five thousand words)

Although it may sound like a lot of words, for me, it comes down to a balance of knowing my why and being energised and motivated to write. If I don't have a writing plan or an end goal, I feel off centre. I make sure I feel energised before I get into my writing chair.

Walking in nature or spending time outside in my back garden watching the morning dawn or dusk fall always boosts my mood. If I'm writing from a different location, I will walk and discover new footpaths and surrounding land which contributes towards new stimulus and ideas.

When I sit down to write, I generally go back to my writing plan or have written up the night before my intention of what I want to cover the next day.

My plans are visually made from post-it notes and fixed on a roll of flip chart paper which is easy to stick to the back of a door and then roll back down again.

I never write by chapter order and sequence and start writing from various sections which feel right for me that day.

When it comes to editing, I may then re-structure content if need be for the best means of writing flow and explore how well chapters fit together.

When working with a publisher or you choose to self-publish, you may have a specific word count to write. If you do, don't let this be your focus instead concentrate on getting good quality content written. You can then negotiate cost, or the editing process will reveal where you need to add to or eliminate word count, content and structure.

I often re-work my projects and check on the order and sequence of the chapters and sub-headings for best fit. I may add in new sections and take others away to be sure the reader is engaged, and there is a variety of information to keep the reader on track.

If I get stuck on writing a specific piece or procrastinate, it's an indication something needs to change. I check in with myself to gauge my emotional mood and notice the internal workings and the chatter of my mind. If my energy is low or I'm overwhelmed, I take time out to re-charge before I write.

I pay attention to what's going on in my home environment, working environment or the world at large. Inner and outer negative stimulus needs to be worked with first to clear the way for writing. WE can lose sight if the end goal if we do not come back to heart, energise and write with the end in mind.

Here I share a basic 'Just Do It Method.' I followed specific routines which helped me effectively structure my time. Every author will have a different opinion on what works for them. You can try out my methods and explore if they are a good fit for you.

Once I clearly defined my end goals of how I want my book to read, and I have established my ideal reader and got clear on what I wanted my book to achieve, only then do I set about writing.

The planning stage of a book can be time-consuming, as can the editing and re-drafting process. The details shared are the writing times aside of research, editing, marketing and advertising. It will be different for every author as to how long it takes to write your first manuscript as we all live different lives with various time constraints. Further on in the writing tips shared, I go into what has worked for me in more detail. For now, it's more important to focus on working through feelings before beginning to make a structured plan to write.

If you feel, however, you have had enough emotional and therapeutic support, and you're ready to commit to writing your book or hire me as a ghostwriter you can find out how I work at www.wendyfry.com

GETTING NAKED WITH YOUR FEELINGS

Every secret of a writer's soul, every experience of his life, every quality of his mind, is written large in his works - Virginia wolf

Writers often struggle with feeling heard; that's why they write. If there ever was a time to get naked with your feelings, this is it. Your journal is ready to hear you out!

Deep inside you, there is a unique voice who yearns for creativity and expression. It may be the voice of your younger self as a child, or perhaps as an adult, you have chosen to keep your feelings within to manage your world, and it has been a coping mechanism. You might hear that voice like a gentle whisper, or, at times, a mighty roar. Keeping your inner author voice suppressed, does not serve you. Whatever your internal voice sounds like now is the time to let it out and in doing so, fully express all of who you are.

Allow yourself to write un-censored, un-masked, de-robed, and be totally outspoken. Together, we will get down to the bare bones of discovering your potential and voice as an author.

Your feelings are your in-built guidance system, designed to let you know when something isn't a good fit for you and to motivate you towards or away from specific experiences.

Most of my clients find until they sit down to write; they weren't previously aware they had been carrying unresolved feelings from the past. Getting naked with your feelings and expressing them in your journal is an opportunity to free yourself from the past and in doing so, create a brighter future.

This section will encourage you to share your thoughts and feelings with your journal. Give your voice permission to release pent-up emotion, within the safety of the processes shared in Write from Your Heart.

Often our attempts at speaking out and revealing true expression were thwarted in childhood. You may have heard phrases like *'children should be seen and not heard', 'keep a stiff upper lip', 'be a brave girl,', 'don't cry', 'pull yourself together', 'don't embarrass me'* and *'respect your elders'.* These are just a few of the possible phrases you may have received when you attempted to express your needs and opinions in childhood and later on life as an adult.

Many adults are still operating from outdated beliefs about what they can say or do before they come to work with me. They find releasing the deluge of emotions in their journal or during a writing retreat is freeing making it easier to get down to the business of writing as an author.

When we push down negative emotions, they fester deep inside and appear in other ways which hurt us.

Writers' block is a classic if we go into our heads and relive the past or worry about the future. Stress, anxiety and depression can impact our writing ability when our hurts and fears are left unaddressed.

When you feel you're up against writer's block or your emotions become overwhelming, take your journal and pour out what you are thinking and how you are feeling.

- Write in the present tense.
- Describe how you feel in the 'now.'
- Notice what changes when you have poured out your heart and soul.
- Then you will be able to get down to the business of writing.

It is often our thoughts which impact our feelings and in turn, limit our writing progress and connection with the heart.

Getting naked with your feelings in your journal before you begin to write your first book will support you into gaining writing momentum and freeing up some emotional space and resilience to write and publish or self-publish your first book.

To aid you in working through your feelings, you have the opportunity to listen to a free guided audio mentioned at the back of this book www.wendyfry.com

REPRESSION – WHAT HAPPENS WHEN WE CAN'T EXPRESS HOW WE FEEL

Unexpressed emotions will never die. They are buried alive and come forth in uglier ways - Sigmund Freud

When we ignore our feelings, our lives become stressful, we are frustrated; this eventually leads to low mood, low energy and possible depression. Having the ability to welcome all emotions and write about them, means we can respond to them and heal what remains unresolved.

Depression *'anger turned inwards'*, otherwise known as *'imploding'*, does not serve us as writers. Stress, anxiety and panic symptoms are common when denial of our feelings or self-expression is marred, or there is fear connected with acknowledging how we feel or speaking up and expressing ourselves.

Please do seek therapeutic support for any overwhelming thoughts and feelings if journaling alone does not boost mood.

ANGER

When we can embrace the full range of human emotions and write about them freely in our journals no longer are, we were eaten alive by what festers within.

Although anger has a bad reputation, it's natural to feel this emotion at some point in your life. When you can vent your feelings through the process of writing, you can reduce many related symptoms of writers' block and lack of writing motivation. Being able to release the anger you may have never spoken or written about how you felt concerning another person's anger can create an emotional shift in your life.

Use the following exercise to explore your memories and perception of anger and importantly, where you may have suppressed anger if you have been told in the past not to express this emotion.

Anger Awareness Writing Exercise

- **Think about your body. When you feel angry, where in your body do you have the sensation of anger the most?**
- **On a scale of 1 to 10, 10 being intense, how high is your anger score?**
- **What's the temperature of your anger?** *(cold, warm, hot, boiling)*
- **If your anger has a colour, what is it?**
- **What texture is your anger?**
- **What shape is your anger?**
- **What is the smell of your anger?**
- **What is the taste of your anger?**
- **Draw your anger; what do you see?**
- **When anger builds up, you may also wish to take physical exercise**
- **Use creative artwork to express your anger**
- **Write about your anger in a journal**

When we grow in maturity and understand ourselves better, we can welcome and face our wrath acknowledging why we feel the way we do, without blame. Simply owning our anger and finding healthy ways to release it is the key to understanding ourselves and expressing ourselves on paper.

EXPLORE MEMORIES OF ANGER

When you can welcome and accept you have a right to be angry, you do not deny your feelings, and you acknowledge all aspects of yourself. Acknowledge your anger by writing about it, let your words flow and then let the anger go.

- **Welcome and accept your anger as you would an old friend**
- **Dig deep and explore why it's there**
- **Recognise anger as being a healthy emotion indicating an opportunity for further healing**
- **Think about what made you angry**
- **How did you respond?**
- **Did you suppress your feelings at the time?**
- **What is your earliest memory of feeling angry?**
- **What unexpressed anger may you have from a previous time which impacts your life now?**

Without full expression, pent-up anger may lead to unhealthy addictive behaviours. Overconsumption of alcohol, drugs, overeating which indirectly serves as a coping mechanism or to dull down emotions you may not know how to express or have been told not to show your anger.

Writing about angry feelings and destructive habits which you know don't serve you in your journal is one of the most cathartic methods available to aid personal expression and heal the hurts within.

Please do make time to write about angry feelings in your journal. It's okay to acknowledge your anger release what you feel, and it will serve you well.

FEAR

Everything you want is on the other side of fear - Jack Canfield

Fear is often misguided. Having the belief something is dangerous (even when it isn't) can make us fearful, including writing and publishing our books.

Fear must be acknowledged to be transformed. When used wisely, fear can be a motivational force.

It helps us to move beyond personal limitations and aids us in developing coping strategies to overcome real or imagined fears.

Writing about fear in the same way you have already written about anger leads to deep inner healing. With your feelings emptied in your journal no longer are those overwhelming emotions trapped inside.

The emotion of fear and anxiety are closely linked. If we are anxious about something, our fear escalates. Fear is a natural impulse when we feel our survival is at threat.

Some worries remain under the surface of conscious awareness and guaranteed when you are sure you want to write and publish your book and voice this fear seems to jump out of nowhere and may frighten you as you grow into expressing yourself as an author. It doesn't have to be this way.

Two acronyms for FEAR are:

Failure to
Experience
Actual
Reality

and

Feeling
Excited
And
Ready

Fear and excitement create similar feelings often sensed in our gut area (solar plexus) so what we perceive as fear, maybe another emotion entirely. With awareness, you can stop your worries escalating.

Exploring Fear Writing Exercise

Invitation

Write about your fears real or perceived in your journal. Below is a list of concerns my clients have shared with me.

Expressing your story publicly

Upsetting your family or caregivers

Perceived opinion, rejection and criticism

Money fears related to writing and publishing your book

Trust issues in yourself and others

Take some time to write about your worries and allow yourself to move beyond your fear-based thinking. Apply this three-step process before or during your journaling time:

- ✓ Thank your fear-based thoughts for being there and acknowledge you realise they are trying to keep you safe (you may like to write a letter to your fear)

- ✓ Remind yourself *'I am not my thoughts.' Write alternative thoughts to counteract fear thoughts and identify the False Evidence Appearing Real.*

- ✓ Replace the negative, fear-based thoughts by re-framing and creating positive empowering thoughts *(Every day in every way, I'm feeling more confident about sharing my thoughts and feelings knowing journaling will help me realise my feelings and emotional overwhelm as well as helping me to write my book)*

Acknowledging and understanding your fears, exploring why they are present, is an important step forward when it comes to transforming your fear and sharing your author voice.

GRIEF & LOSS

Grief and loss are something we will all experience.

If you are separated from someone or something or indeed experiencing grief and loss through bereavement, you may experience disturbed sleep patterns, changeable appetite, disbelief, shock, numbness and the emotions of anger, guilt and, sadness.

You may find it almost impossible to stop thinking about the person or the loss in question. Writing about the full range of emotions which surface will serve you well.

Writing about what we hoped for, what we have lived through using the theme of grief in your book can make for compelling reading.

Strategies to overcome your grief and loss are:

- ✓ **Journaling freely with expressive writing**
- ✓ **Working towards accepting your loss and talking about it**
- ✓ **Understanding your perception of loss and how you think act and feel about it**
- ✓ **Writing a book about how you have overcome your grief and the processes you used to help you through**

This section is a short overview of some of the emotions experienced and how journaling can support you in releasing overwhelming feelings. Please so seek therapeutic support if journaling alone does not improve your mood.

GUILT

Anger has a twin sister, and her name is guilt. When you feel guilty it is a voice inside of you saying "I feel I've been unfair to someone"- Calvin D Banyan - The Secret Language of Feelings

It is possible to turn guilt into personal growth. Instead of guilty feelings limiting you, you can explore what made you do what you did. If in hindsight, you wish you had acted differently, this is an opportunity to learn from the experience. Reflecting in this way, you know you could have made a different choice or taken a separate action, though, at the *time* of making your decision, you did not have the awareness or learning in place.

Guilt, like anger and grief, can be overcome, healed and transformed. Going over an event and berating yourself for something you could have done but didn't - or did do but wish you hadn't, serves no purpose. Forgiving yourself for your actions, behaviours and consequences, will aid you in moving beyond your current limitations.

What makes you feel guilty?

Think about some of the rules and conditions imposed upon you growing up. What was ok or not ok for you? (Guilt links with what we believe or told we should consider, is moral or immoral)

How many of these examples bring up guilt for you?

Write about your feelings of guilt in your journal

Invitation

- **Things you've said or done in the past**
- **Making a choice which went against someone else's beliefs about what they believed was right for you**
- **Believing you have caused another person suffering**
- **Saying no to others**
- **Arguing or disagreeing with someone**
- **Standing up for yourself**
- **Setting boundaries**
- **Lying about how you spend your time**
- **Not calling when you said you would**
- **Not wanting to visit a friend or family member**
- **Not liking or loving someone despite your best efforts**

- **Not wanting to follow someone else's rules**
- **Being angry at yourself or another person**
- **Choosing to be estranged from a friend or family member**
- **Feeling responsible for others and not wanting to be**
- **Resenting someone's illness, situation or lifestyle**
- **Not being fully present in a relationship or being unfaithful**
- **Not wanting to be someone's carer**
- **Wishing someone who hurt you would die**
- **Believing you caused someone's death**
- **Not telling someone you loved them before they died**
- **Not trying to repair a relationship**

Your perception of guilt may change and lessen over time. Journaling helps to ease the feeling of guilt aiding catharsis and release.When you can forgive yourself and recognise you did all you could with the internal resources you had, your outlook becomes more balanced.

REGRET

Never look back unless you are planning to go that way - Henry David Thoreau

Regrets, we all have them. Even Frank Sinatra in his song *'I Did It My Way'* sings about regret, but the ultimate message is how he did things his way to live his life to the full and be all of whom could be. We could each learn a lesson from Frank.

Regret is a natural part of life. On reflection, we may make a different decision armed with the knowledge, learning, wisdom and experience we have now. We make choices at points in our lives when those appear to be the only apparent options. There may have been nothing else we could have done differently at the time to change our circumstances then or now, and we need to accept that we were doing the best we could at the time. Self- forgiveness plays a part in moving on from regret and merely using the experience as a learning opportunity.

I like to think of regrets, as the *'If Only' syndrome*. If only I had done or said this or that. We allow guilt, regret, shame and anger rule our lives if we spend too long playing the *'if only'* game.

Use the invitation below as a starting point for your journaling process to aid emotional catharsis copying out the introduction statements and adding your endings.

Writing Release Exercise

Invitation

- If only I had
- If only I hadn't
- If only I did
- If only I didn't
- If only I'd asked
- If only I'd said
- If only I'd listened
- If only I were
- If only I weren't
- If only I'd done
- If only I'd been
- If only I'd told her
- If only I knew
- If only she
- If only we'd
- If only I could

- **If only I'd learnt**
- **If only things were different**

It's natural to have regrets when we focus on what we could have done differently in the past. The problem is we judge ourselves harshly as to why we made individual choices.

Guilt, like any emotion, can range in intensity. If we are not able to move beyond the past, accept ourselves and our faults we remain powerless, guilt becomes more prominent than the event which caused the original feeling.

SADNESS

If you don't think your anxiety, depression, sadness and stress impact your physical health, think again. All these emotions trigger chemical reactions in your body, which can lead to inflammation and a weakened immune system - Kris Carr

To avoid feeling sad, we bury the emotion of grief in the same way we might also bury our anger. If we have been taught not to show our feelings and find ourselves unable to communicate, express opinion or concern - the sadness stays inside us lurks waiting to be triggered.

It is worth reflecting on why you may previously have hidden your sadness and the meaning you place on being able to express your sorrow. Grief, as well as anger, can be labelled as a negative emotion and one society says we should not display. In truth, a healthy expression of anger and sadness would serve us all far better than keeping it inside. Your journal is waiting, and you can share all you wish to from your heart in relations to your sadness.

Owning up to and acknowledging your sadness is one of the most difficult human experiences you may ever face. If you have been taught not to express your feelings, the grief you experience deep within may never be processed - leaving you with a sense of melancholy and sadness, as you go through life.

Children do not always know how to process and release the emotion of sadness; we learn from our parents and caregivers. By addressing our feelings as adults and acknowledging what made us sad in childhood and later years, we can heal old hurts.

With this awareness, we can move on from feeling resentful and holding onto memories which are painful and keep us feeling small.

Use the following exercise to release sadness, expressing your thoughts, feelings and emotions in your journal.

Letting Go of Sadness Writing Exercise

Invitation

- **What makes you sad?**
- **What did you learn about the emotion of sadness growing up?**
- **How often have you been soothed by others when you were sad?**
- **When you cried or showed emotion for whatever reason, how were you responded to?**

- **How do the people you are close to express their sadness?**
- **When do you deny your sadness?**
- **When others show sadness through crying and communicating how they feel, how do you respond?**

Dealing with sadness is a natural part of life. Your journal will support you to process and release your feelings fully.

There may be times when something or someone, triggers off one of the beliefs or emotions mentioned, and it may require you to do some extensive journaling on these themes. If you are concerned about the strength of your feelings, I recommend you work with a trained therapist, to help you to understand and release the build-up of emotion.

When you can review and re-frame the meaning, you place on your feelings, and you can recognise when your judgement may have been deleting, distorting or generalising information it becomes easier to understand your behaviours and responses when triggered.

Becoming more objective and re-evaluating your thoughts, feelings and emotions, is a great way to place new meaning on your experience.

RE-SETTING YOUR FOCUS

Between stimulus and response, there is a space. In that space is our power to choose our response. In our response lies our growth and our freedom - Victor E. Frankl

Apply the following writing exercise to reset your focus and gain clarity on your writing journey ahead.

Invitation

- **Write down a list of the thought patterns and feelings you experience most often**
- **In a column alongside these feelings, you might like to look for counterevidence and record the positive feelings you have (i.e. appreciation, love, connection, gratitude for your life etc.)**
- **Completing this exercise will help you to reframe your focus and get in touch with the more positive aspects of your situation**
- **Keep going with this exercise, until the positive list is longer than the negative**

THOUGHT PATTERNS

Become aware of your automatic negative thought patterns which get in the way of writing freely. You may wish to journal them out and explore them fully.

I've listed some examples which get in the way of heart-based writing. The mind takes over, and 'heart-speak' gets left behind.

Highlight or write out in your journal the thought patterns, which are the most common for you and write down your intention as to how you will address and re-frame your thinking.

Bringing Balance to Your Thinking Writing Exercise

Invitation

- **Mind reading** - you assume you know what others are thinking without having any evidence
- **Fortune telling** - you predict the future negatively
- **Catastrophising** - you believe what has happened or will happen with will be so awful and unbearable you won't be able to stand it

- **Labelling** - you give negative traits to yourself and others, ignoring the positives
- **Negative filtering** - you focus on the negative aspect of your experiences and do not notice the positives
- **Over generalising** - you see a global pattern of negatives based on a single incident with your mother
- ***'Shoulds'***- you see events in terms of how things 'should' be, rather than merely focusing on what is
- **Personalising** - you assume an unreasonable amount of blame for adverse events
- **Blaming** - you focus on blaming others as the source of your negative feelings
- **Unfair comparisons** - you interpret events in terms of standards that are unrealistic when you compare yourself to others
- **Regret orientation** - you focus on ways you could have done better in the past, rather than on what you can do better now
- **Emotional reasoning** - you let your past feelings guide your interpretation of reality
- **Inability to disconfirm** - you reject any evidence or arguments which might contradict your negative thoughts

- **Judgement focus** - you view yourself and past events, in terms of good-bad or superior-inferior, rather than merely describing, accepting or understanding things to be the way they are. You are focused on the judgement of others, as well as on your views you place on yourself

Negative emotions like loneliness, envy, and guilt have an immortal role to play in a happy life: they're big, flashing signs something needs to change - Gretchen Rubin

WHAT ARE YOU CHOOSING?

Don't live someone else's life. Don't be trapped by the dogma, which is living with the results of other people's thinking. And most important have the courage to follow your heart and intuition. Everything else is secondary - Steve Jobbs

As we continue to move through this Journaling Invitation, you will gain new ideas about the various processes I use in my personal development and coaching those I work with, whether that be as an aspiring author or for therapeutic and emotional support.

I have used the method shared below personally and professionally in my mentoring programmes. You may wish to explore and test this idea taking full responsibility for any outcome or choice you may decide to make. Remember if a decision once established does not suit you once you have explored it thoroughly, choose again. Every opportunity brings with it insightful learning.

MAKING DECISIONS – EXPLORATION FOR CONTINUED WRITING & JOURNALING

A writer is a world trapped in a person - Victor Hugo

When was the last time you made a decision only to regret it later?

Do you have a current or future choice to make?

Before completing the following writing exercise, you may like to journal about the areas of your life where you've made decisions you now regret and indeed those decisions made which have served you well.

Invitation

1. **Take all choices concerning the decision**
2. **Write them up as individual words or a short paragraph on a post-it-note of the same colour and size**
3. **Fold the different pieces of paper up with words inside and not visible**
4. **Hold your hands together with pieces of paper collectively together in front of the heart centre**

5. Ask for insight into the best choice for you
6. Shake up the pieces of paper together in hands
7. Lay them out on a table or clear area
8. Pick one piece of paper at a time
9. Walk around the room a few times with it, notice all your senses
10. Feel into the paper in your closed hands
11. Breathe in and allow the sensory data from the paper to flow through to you without reading
12. Take your hands and the paper to your heart centre reflecting on this individual choice
13. Notice your posture
14. Speed of walk
15. Stature
16. Mood
17. Feeling
18. Thoughts/insights
19. Energy level
20. What does this decision feel like for you?
21. Write about it in your journal (do not yet open the choice)

22. **Break state between each question and selection by drinking water, going to the toilet, saying your telephone number backwards or moving from the room you are in for a moment**

~~~~~~

- Repeat the exercise as shown as and when you wish to gain insight
- Go through all the choices and options making notes remembering to break state between
- Which choice do you sense in the best?
- What choice lifts, you, makes you feel positive, confident, joyous? What decision do you intuitively 'know' this is the right choice?
- Open the 'right choice' piece of paper. What does it say, how do you feel when you open it? Are you disappointed the other choices were not the answer you thought you would have? Write about your learnings in your journal

Using this process, it drops you out of your mind and into your heart to gain sensory acuity. You move away from head-based thinking and 'trying' to make a rational decision with the mind alone.

I believe the 'sensed energy 'comes into the intuitive heart as an information stream. It takes the head based, thinking out of the way when we connect in
~~~~~~

with our hearts offering a more harmonious outcome which is in alignment with the heart.

Some may compare this exercise to muscle testing using kinesiology or dowsing methods, postural sway and pendulum testing. You may wish to research further on these methods for reading energy data as I call it if this is something of interest to you.

I can't tell you exactly how this exercise works scientifically. I only know it's helped the many people I have worked with making better choices than with thought alone.

There are many ways to decide on a possible outcome. You may wish to use this exercise as 'entertainment value only' and be curious about what this method brings up for you. It does not guarantee results and is a light-hearted offering for your exploration. Always go with the techniques you feel are right for you and take actions only when considering your personal choice responsibly and the long-term impact in doing so.

INTENTION – REMEMBERING YOUR WHY

As you live deeper in the heart, the mirror gets clearer and clearer – Rumi

What's your why? What makes you want to write?

Up to now, you may not have considered why you'd like to share your unique voice. It will be helpful to you to understand 'your why' from the outset. Your inspiration to write can be your ultimate motivational tool when you begin every journal exercise, blog, book or writing format of your choice.

Write out in your journal all the reasons you want to write. I have included some ideas to get you started.

Invitation

- **Writing for enjoyment**
- **Journaling to heal**
- **Writing for personal reflection**
- **Journaling to express your truth**
- **Writing to educate and inspire**
- **Recording life experience**

- **Writing for catharsis**
- **Journaling to overcoming difficulties**
- **Writing for self-expression**
- **Changing behaviours to get in the habit of writing**
- **Writing to gain clarity and insight**
- **Journaling to understand patterns and behaviours**
- **Writing to create something tangible**
- **Write your first book or complete the one you've started**

Your why and your reasons to write may change over time. My need for journaling helps me express my truth, aids for emotional catharsis, and now when I am free of overwhelming emotions, I love to write and create. As with all my writing, it is my hope I inspire others to discover their authentic voice and write from the heart.

JOURNALING INVITATIONS AND PROMPTS

When you write freely from your heart, you will discover your authentic voice within – Wendy Fry

Whether you write first thing in the morning, the last thing at night, on the train, while waiting to pick your kids up from school, it only matters now where you write but that you write.

You may squeeze in time to write in your lunch break, locked in the toilet, by torchlight under the covers or you can find a delightful place in nature to be inspired.

Once you begin journaling, you will find writing becomes a healthy addiction, and you can't get enough of it.

1. **You learn to write by writing**
2. **Write regularly**
3. **Write uncensored**
4. **Leave editing and punctuation to the end**
5. **Think, speak, act, and write like an author, own your words and your space**
6. **Use your journal to express your voice and share what needs to be said**
7. **Find out what you want to write about**

8. **What's your vision, your end goal, your motivation to write?**
9. **Take Inspired action and write about what you love**
10. **Keep a journal at home and by your bedside**
11. **Take a notebook or paper and pen with you wherever you go**
12. **Make lists or bullet points for speed and ease**
13. **Write letters which you don't send**
14. **Compose poetry and prose**
15. **Scrawl ideas on the back of napkins and beer mats**
16. **Jot down ideas**
17. **Doodle ideas visually and then write about them**
18. **Sketch, paint, create something and then write about it**

Raise your energy in whichever way you love to get motivated, i.e. dancing, running, gardening, music, hiking in the great outdoors. Any high vibe activity which gives you an energy boost is perfect for getting you into writer's flow.

ON LIFE AND LIVING

On a scale of one to ten, ten being you are living life fully and on your terms, how closely are you living your ideal life?

How much commitment followed by inspired action do you take to achieve what you believe will give you a sense of long-term happiness, contentment and wholeness?

I invite you to answer these questions in your journal and write about what comes to heart and mind.

Invitation

- **Are you genuinely taking decisive action to reach your highest potential?**
- **What areas of your life need improvement?**
- **Where may you be overextending yourself?**
- **What stops you writing or limits your time to write?**
- **How often do you agree to do something you don't want to?**

- **What choices can you make to improve the life areas of your life which are vital for you to develop?**
- **Consider what you need to start doing, stop doing or do differently to change your life and find time to write**

It's helpful to gauge what areas of your life may benefit from a change. You can explore the following life areas in your journal. Detail, what needs improvement, the areas of your life you'd like to add to

Note too which categories support your time to journal and to begin writing or start completing your first book or book series and which categories get in the way.

a) Assess the amount of attention you're currently devoting to each area of your life. Some examples - Health, Friends and Family, Partner and Relationships, Physical Environment, Fun and Recreation, Personal or Spiritual Development, Career, Money & Finances. Be aware; your life areas will need different levels of attention at different times. Consider each area in turn, write about the amount of care you're devoting to that area of your life.

b) Notice where some areas have no attention, less time commitment from you or too much focus

c) How balanced is your life? What needs to change?

d) Next, it's time to consider your ideal in each area of your life to create more balance. Inevitably you will need to make choices and compromises if you want to write a book, you need to make time to do so and consider which areas of your life are taking your attention.

e) What areas need to be balanced out? How will your life be different when you've dedicated more time to write?

f) Make a daily, weekly and monthly plan to factor in firstly the journaling process, and when you are in the habit of writing you can extend the time to write your book

There are likely areas stealing your time to write and others which will benefit from reprioritising your commitment and time. Completing this exercise helps you focus on work-life balance and making time to write your first book.

Some aspiring authors are too busy to write with demanding professional and family life. Because they are serious about writing a book to advance their career, status, leave a legacy or some other reason, they employ my services as a ghost-writer to write for them. I love this way of working, keeping the author's name on the page and working for them to share their message.

If you're not able to invest in my services and hire me as your ghostwriter and you want to write your own story and transformational book, you must commit dedicated time to write. It's essential if you intend to write and publish your book within a specific time frame you set appropriate boundaries. Saying no is much easier than you may think as are changing the habits of a lifetime.

If there are areas of your life where you are overextending yourself, it's time to make a change. Make your words and your story matter. Say no to what doesn't serve you and yes to writing your first book.

Once you have identified the life areas that need attention, it's time to set yourself smart goals and plan the actions required to work on restoring or creating balance.

SMART MOVES AND SMART GOALS

Taking part in this exercise will show the areas of your life, which need your attention and bring your insight into what isn't working and encouragement to work towards achieving whole life balance. If you become too focused on one life area, other areas suffer.

Invitation

Today's Date:

Review Date: 6 months from now:

S - specific, significant, stretching

M - measurable, meaningful, motivational

A - attainable, achievable, acceptable, action-oriented

R - realistic, relevant, reasonable, rewarding, results-oriented

T - time-based, timely, tangible, trackable

When you set goals and aims, it's important to remember what the advantages and disadvantages of these goals bring.

Starting with the neglected areas, what do you need to start doing to regain balance?

In the areas that currently sap your energy and time, what can you stop doing or delegate to someone else?

What can you do differently to make your writing life work for you?

Commit to the action steps which contribute to your overall goals using the smart moves and smart goals exercise.

Writing your goals down, taking action and reviewing your progress is a smart move and will aid you in completing your first book.

PART SEVEN

'WRITE' FRAME OF MIND

'WRITE' FRAME OF MIND

It's all right. It's over. It was just a memory - J.K Rowling, Harry Potter and the Chamber of Secrets

This chapter focuses on getting you into the 'write frame of mind. 'That's right, and this isn't a typo, it's a play on words.

When we focus on writing quality content with precise, focused attention, beginning with daily journaling, it stretches you and allows you to learn new behaviours to write from your heart with your first book in mind.

Our past determines our future, negatively if we allow it. Unless we explore how we remember what happened to us, we may never move forward in life. By understanding the meanings and judgements, we place on ourselves because of the experiences we have lived through we realise being aware of the past is helpful, living there Isn't.

I wouldn't change my past for anything. It has made me who I am today. In what way may your past have shaped you for the greater good? Think about it now. Write about your past. What makes you, you because of the life you've lived?

Living the unexamined and unwritten life, we may continue to live in the past to the detriment of our future and all we can be, do and have.

It's never too late to pick up your journal where you left off. You can write out what happened, what you wish had happened and indeed how your past has shaped you positively. Writing about hardships and what we have overcome is freeing. Our past need not negatively determine our future. We each can write your future into being.

On another note, writing about what you love, appreciate and enjoy about your past and your life journey so far, positive memory recall boost's mood, raises energy and ramps up your power to write. Journaling is about creating a delicate balance between what needs to be released before you write your first book and to explore what to include and what to leave out.

We are all different when it comes to journaling. Choose what works for you. Go inside your heart and ask ''what do you need to write through me?'' Listen deeply, and your heart will guide you.

WRITING FREELY

Sometimes known as 'Stream of Conscious Writing,' this way of expressing yourself enables you to become aware of your self-talk and the inner workings of your mind. Writing by hand freely in your journal spring cleans your mind and in doing so allows you to go deeper into your heart and the true essence of you.

You may choose to focus on a specific theme and write about your past, present or future. It's also perfectly okay to write about what comes into your mind as you begin your journal page, curious as to where it takes you.

Invitation

The following is an example of one of the ways you can write freely.

1. Choose a time each day where you can write uninterrupted for ten to fifteen minutes
2. Have your journal or loose sheets of paper to hand and a pen or pencil
3. Write non-stop. If you think you don't have anything to write about and are stuck in any

way, write about how you feel even if you write ''I don't know what to write about'' and then see what comes up as you write about not being able to write

4. Let your thoughts flow and dump them out on the page uncensored. The good, the bad and the ugly are all welcome in your journal
5. You may write about things you haven't spoken about to gain a healing opportunity
6. Write quickly without considering punctuation or grammar, let your inner dialogue flow
7. Stop writing ideally when your thoughts dry up or if you are pressed for time, stop at the end of the ideal writing time frame which you set.
8. If emotions become overwhelming when you write, take a break, do something different for a short amount of time to change your emotional state, re-energise to boost your mood.
9. Come back to your journal and read what you have written. What do you notice? What themes and topics have come up for you? On comparing journal entries, what patterns and ideas are present for you?
10. Be aware if there is a specific event, memory, missing event or future fear which may benefit from further journaling

11. For some writers, they prefer to destroy the pages written; for others, they use their journal as a means of comparison to see how far they have come in the journaling process. Other writers use their journals for storytelling, writing their first book or blog or indeed turning their life experience into a memoir series

12. Continue regularly with this method of writing freely. There is no limit on the amount you write, and you can set a more extended period aside or even schedule out diary dates and times for yourself and have a writing day or retreat.

AUTOMATIC AND INTUITIVE WRITING

This is the voice of your journal speaking- '' All your life, I mean ALL of it, is welcome here. A haven, a place where you can write down your hopes and fears. Between my pages permit yourself to unburden yourself, release your grief, share your guilt and heal your shame. Let go of your pain and anger and the dark nights of your soul. Tell me everything. I am here for you." – Wendy Fry

In the 1800s, people first became aware of the automatic writing phenomenon. It became more popular in the 1900s. There are different schools of thought about what it is and how to do it. This way of writing is possibly the most effective when you need to gain direction and insight around a possible problem, choice or decision.

When writing automatically, Information comes through from the ''higher self.'' Many people believe to write automatically is a form of channelled writing which comes through spirit and someone no longer on the earthly plane. Others suggest a connection with God, The Universe or a spirit entity writing through us. Predictions and prophecies are often intuitively written by gaining access to an energy stream and energetic data.

Spiritualists, psychics and mediums may record the words which come through writing by hand with pen and paper, audio recording, typing on a computer or using an Ouija board.

I don't class myself to be a psychic though I have been told I am clairaudient by a psychic friend of mine. If you're not familiar with what clairaudient means it means I hear the messages come into my awareness in audio, spoken in my own voice or the voice of another. I often receive downloads and insights when I'm working with clients and going through the 'Define Your Ideal Reader Breakthrough Blueprint' consultation helping them to gain clarity around writing their book and sharing their message. I trust entirely the intuitive information which comes through and freely share my insights with those who are open to receiving these communications.

When we allow ourselves to seek a spiritual connection by whatever form or information stream it comes through, you will find you can easily access this way of writing. The more you write this way, the more comfortable you will become by doing so.

My suggestion for this process is to find a quiet place to sit, breathe deeply and focus inwards to still the rush of the world around you. You may like to light a candle and create a sacred space of some kind before you set the intention to connect in spirit and begin your channelled writing.

There is much information to glean from the energy stream. Messages may come through to you from wherever you believe they are to be available. There is nothing to fear; writing this way takes out the 'how to write' and you write by channelled means.

I am doing it right now as I write, I still my mind and connect with my heart. The information comes through by auditory means, and I trust myself to write it.

Writing this way isn't about perfect composition or grammar; you allow the content already 'there' in the information data stream to come through.

Determine the way you wish to record your automatic writing whether that be in your journal, A4 paper or on your laptop or pc. Have these items to hand being ready to start writing when the downloads come through.

To support you in writing this way, I have detailed the process and have listed some possible questions to ask yourself. Allow the ideas posed to stimulate automatic writing.

Some of my clients like to use two different coloured pens to form a clear question and answer process when reviewing their journal and then later giving the information time to settle.

Intuitive Writing Exercise

Invitation

1. What area of your life do you wish to gain insight?
2. Pick your question from this list or devise your own
3. Write it down on the top of your journal or piece of paper
4. Sit quietly or meditate
5. You may wish to close your eyes
6. Calmly focus inward
7. Tune out the sounds around you
8. Breathe slowly taking deep and easy breaths
9. Allow your mind to go blank
10. In the stillness gained you may wish to form an imaginary bridge between yourself and the source you wish to connect with to gain information (The Universe, Spirit, God etc.)

11. **Ask open questions aloud or inside your mind**
12. **Write down the answers which come into your awareness**
13. **Be open to how you experience the information through your senses. Pay attention to the visuals, your feelings, the smells, tastes, and what you hear. Notice your physical and emotional response as this information comes to you.**
14. **Come back to what you have written perhaps an hour after each sitting**
15. **Reflect on your writing**
16. **How will using the information gained by writing this way help you move forward with your life?**
17. **What insights do you learn?**
18. **What action will you take based on your insights.?**

Automatic, Intuitive writing is profound and can be developed with practice. Also, you may like to extend your writing practice by asking the following questions in your journal.

Ask yourself these questions:

- ✓ What do I need to know today?
- ✓ What do you need to write through me?

- ✓ Why do I feel stuck, confused, discouraged, etc.?
- ✓ What may be blocking me from achieving my goals?
- ✓ How can I improve my situation?
- ✓ What am I here to learn?
- ✓ What is my purpose?
- ✓ How can I create more balance in my life?
- ✓ What steps can I take to improve my career, relationships, health, personal life, etc.?
- ✓ What is the best course of action regarding…?
- ✓ How can I make money doing what I love?
- ✓ What am I missing or not seeing clearly?
- ✓ Tell me what I need to know about this specific person or situation?

YOUR LIFE IN THREE ACTS

When we deny the story, it defines us. When we can own the story, we can write a brave new ending - Breneé Brown

Invitation

This writing invitation has no strict rules. Simply write about your life past, present and future in three acts.

Consider the subtitles, characters and the actors you will have as the stars of your show if you wish to extend your writing piece.

When I offer this exercise in my writing groups, there is often much hilarity at the titles and the realisation at the state of one's life if left unaddressed.

You can have fun with this and write it as a fiction setting or indeed a factual piece.

POETRY IN MOTION

Writing is the first step to becoming an author. Whether it's continued journaling, starting a blog or writing poetry every day is a great day to get down to the business of writing - Wendy Fry

How and what you choose to write in your journal is entirely up to you. You may wish to use rhyming poetry, sonnets, Haiku type poems. Villanelle, Cinquains, or Epic poetry. The three most common type of poetry is Lyric, narrative and dramatic. Free verse poetry and Acrostic are my favourites.

You may like to take some time researching and trying out the various methods of poetry writing and set aside time for a poetry journal in addition to other types of journaling processes.

I have included here the extended version of the earlier poem *'This is Your Journal Speaking.'*

This is Your Journal Speaking

I see you there
I feel you
I already know you more
Then you know yourself
I have been waiting for you
I'm so pleased we found each other
I am ready to listen
To your happy memories
Your magical moments
Your Wins
Those successes you play down
It's about time you spoke of
These special times
Write about those beautiful things
You thought you had forgotten
You will remember them easily
Just by reading my words
Those wonderful memories
Will flood into your heart and mind
I want to know of your aspirations
To understand your hopes
To help you
Actualise
Your dreams
Please share with me
What and who you love
Tell me
What keeps you make at night

In a positive way?
Don't keep the fun stuff
To yourself
Share ALL of it with me
The highs
The lows
The in-betweens
And,
Remember
I have your back
I am here for you
I am beside you on this journey
We walk as one
We are in this together
I want you to know you intimately
In-to-me-see
I am here for you
As deep as you think you can go
I will invite you to dive
Even deeper
Because you can
With me
I am your confidante
Your trusted friend
I can be
Whatever or whoever
You want me to be
I am your journal
I want you to know

I love you
I always have
And always will
I'm so pleased
You have found me
In turn
You
Will discover
YOU
and
ALL
You
Can
Become
The time is now
It's time
To
Write
From
Your
Heart

EARTH ENERGY

Every day is an opportunity to write from your heart - Wendy Fry

Many people tell me that they feel lost. They may have a good life on the surface, but somehow, they are not connected to their purpose, their reason for being, without which life is empty.

This exercise is written by Anne Jirsch Author of Future Vision Your Working Life – Strategies to help you get ahead

This exercise will align you to our beautiful planet and its own special vibration aiding your writing and creative energy flow.

Connecting with the Earth's Energy Vibration

Invitation

Imagine you are standing out in nature on a beautiful day. Stand tall and be aware of the ground beneath your feet. Take time to focus on your surroundings on this beautiful planet, become aware of the vast oceans and seas, the mountains, forests, jungles and deserts, the cities, the towns and villages. Be conscious of all the people and creatures that live upon the earth and know that everything has a part to play, even the tiniest insect.

Know that the earth is a form of energy and has a consciousness of its own.

Feel the aliveness of the planet and notice how it has its unique vibration, it is subtle but stop for a moment to be still and mindful, and you will feel it.

As you connect to the vibration of the earth, your vibration will strengthen.

Now allow your energy to flow down into the earth blending with the earth's vibration.

As your energy flows down to the earth, feel the earth energy flow back up to you.

Now allow your aura to grow bigger and bigger and brighter and brighter until it is flowing around the entire earth sending radiant energy for the good of all.

Just know that as your energy flows outwards, it will positively influence others and I, in turn, they influence even more people. The ripple effect will spread further and further.

Know that every positive thought and action that you make will ripple out to others and down to the centre of the earth, down to the deepest point on earth that will then flow outwards to every inch of the planet.

Your vibration will flow to the past and the future creating more and more positive vibrations, influencing people everywhere; the four corners of the earth, the past and future. You are flowing energy to your ancestors and those still to be born in the future.

It will flow into the universe where it will carry on creating positive energy for infinity.

As you stand upon the earth, know that your smallest contribution will make a difference. It will do more than you can ever imagine.

Write about your experience of reading through and utilising the above exercise in your journal.

WRITE FROM YOUR HEART

Put your thoughts to sleep. Do not let them cast a shadow over the moon of your heart - let go of thinking - Rumi

Becoming future-focused using the various exercises in Write from Your Heart moves you away from the pain of the past. While being in the moment is important, it's equally important as an author to have the ability to plan and work to deadlines or 'live-lines' as I prefer to call them.

Creating a Positive Future

1. Place your hands directly over the centre of your chest (heart chakra) fingers extending to your heart, laying one hand flat on top of the other. If you prefer, put your hands one on top of the other in the centre of your chest. Laying your hands on your physical body, thus 'the energy body' helps to not only stabilise the heart it also connects you with your heart's innate intelligence and information centre.

2. Take deep breaths in and out through your nose or mouth as preferred. Slow down your breathing down, taking the breath down to your stomach area. When breathing in this way and slowing down your breathing, you stimulate the relaxation response. A deeper breath can be noted by your stomach, which will expand on breathing in and on breathing out decrease the distension. Breathing this way has many health as well as emotional benefits.
3. Take your heart and mind to the future. To the perfect place in time and space where you hold your book of words in your hand
4. What do you notice?
5. What colour is your book cover, the title, the image on the cover?
6. Where were you?
7. What was the event or occasion?
8. Are you alone or with others?
9. What is the time of day, the month year?
10. What do you see, hear, feel, smell, taste and sense?
11. Turn those feelings up. Take continued deep breaths in and out. Allow the sensory experience to rise within you. Remember the 'data energy' the information which comes back to you which is in your internal storage system of thoughts, feelings, emotions and senses - enjoy!

12. Write down your experiences in your journal.
13. It's beautiful to write your future into being in your journal in detail. Engaging in future creation and manifestation empowers each one of us to know the opportunities writing our books can bring
14. Repeat as and when needed.

TRANSFORMING YOUR FUTURE

Future Life Progression, pioneered by Anne Jirsch author of 'Future Vision Your Working Life, 'is a unique and safe way to look ahead into your future to find out what next steps to take in your life NOW!

Benefits of FLP

- ✓ It's a positive experience that can only change your life for the better!
- ✓ Imagine what would it be like to have clarity over the decisions you need to make
- ✓ How would gaining insight into your future aid you in overcoming the challenges you have right now?

FLP is perfect if you are you:

- ✓ **Undecided if a particular choice is a right decision?**
- ✓ **Confused if a specific job or relationship right for you?**
- ✓ **Need clarity if a specific house move is the best move?**
- ✓ **Want to know when is the right time to make an investment or launch a new business?**
- ✓ **Fed up with the same old same old and want to change?**
- ✓ **Are you overwhelmed?**

'The Future You' has already resolved your problems and knows the answers to your questions. Future Life Progression takes you on a sensory journey where you will move you forward in time to solve any current problems you may be experiencing now whether these are writing-related or otherwise.

FLP offers insights into living your life with purpose rather than 'going through the motions', feeling stuck or letting life pass by.

My clients love this way of working as it's a positive experience and offers a learning opportunity into making the rest of your life the best of your life as well as exploring those all-important book titles and content you are going on to write!

Here are just a few of the many ways to experience FLP

- ✓ **Future Life Progression** ~ Moving to a time frame of your choice say 5 or 10 years
- ✓ **Alternate Futures** ~ Taking you through a variety of future options (this is great for making decisions)
- ✓ **Alternative Lifetimes** ~ moving beyond your current life to your highly evolved future self
- ✓ **Your Best Year in Business** ~ Find your most successful future in precisely a year

Since seeing my future as an author and speaker many years ago, it has enabled me to take action in the direction of my dreams. I simply caught up with my future self and made things happen in a shorter time frame. How you use the information in your own future life progression session is entirely up to you.

I have been fortunate to have my work using FLP featured in Natural Health Magazine June 2013

Soul and Destiny magazine in April 2013. Interviews at Oxford TV have allowed me to talk about my experience using this modality.

Here's what others are saying after experiencing Future life Progression for the first time:

" Future Life Progression is a beautiful process; it's gentle in its approach and allows you to gain a better understanding of what might be holding you back from starting or completing your book. It's an opportunity to let go of the past, to learn and to feel inspired and invigorated in the present and for the future" ~ *Chris*

"I am setting up a new business with my first book as a foundation from training courses, so my focus was on how my business would progress over the next 5 and 10 years. I found the insight I gained from this session quite invaluable.

I had many ideas regarding the direction my life would take. This session has helped me to streamline my thoughts and focus on one path. Looking back, it is now quite obvious what I should have been doing, but, in my confusion, I just couldn't see it. I would recommend this to anyone who is looking for some direction in life" ~ Rose

" I have to say I was blown away by the clarity the outcomes the process facilitated. Wendy took me on a guided tour of my future life and critical moments that lie ahead. A compelling future lay before me which both motivated and inspired me. I gained profound insights into future possibilities along with raising questions about how to bridge the gap from where I am to where my future appears to be. I really identified with the emotions and feeling the process elicited and know that many would benefit from stepping into the future in the way this process provides" ~ Stefan

" I felt empowered by the information I learned, and it seemed to 'make sense' on some deep level. I was also astonished about how connected to other themes it was. Also, how precise the information was that I received for the titles of my books" ~ Deborah

" Several days later, I still hold on to the imagery for the covers of my books and the lessons I learned in my FLP session will help me set boundaries and make a writing plan. Wendy holds the space to allow for a calm and very relaxed session. I feel

very safe to be myself with Wendy's FLP and writing coaching. I have finally been able to share my story. I wish I'd started writing sooner" ~ Peter

" Wendy and I worked on a relationship which was getting in the way of writing and expanding my business. My presenting problem was not being able to stand on my own two feet as an independent woman. Wendy took me back to a past life of being in chains around my neck and lots of strong cotton cords. We then proceeded to cut the cords and release me from my neck chains.

This plays out in my life by my beliefs that I need a man to help me with my finances. Even if the current conditions are not constructive and healthy. Future learnings where I am now free from the prison I was confined to. I am no longer chained to past circumstances. Being able to see myself in two years standing on my own two feet and feeling free and calm and living within my own skin was liberating. A compelling session. Thank you" ~ Darlene

✓ Ready to gain insights into the best career for you?

✓ Want to know the title of your first book?

✓ Need confirmation that you're in the right relationship?

✓ Simply need to know if a choice you are considering is the right choice.

Future Life Progression will lead the way offering you clarity and insights into your life in general and your best possible future as an author.

You can book your chosen FLP session at www.wendyfry.com.

Do something today your 'Future Self'

will thank you for!

AUTHOR TIPS REVEALED

My first book Find YOU, Find LOVE here's what I did:

- Visually, I planned on post-it notes the chapter outline and order flow.
- Got up an hour earlier
- Did a full forty-five-minute Qi Gong routine to raise energy and clear my mind
- Turned off social media, emails, phone or other distractions (all were left off until I'd completed the word count, topic, chapter or content I had aimed to create for that day)
- I wrote every day whether it was an hour, 4 hours or 20 minutes and completed my book within six months
- I set boundaries and let friends and family know I was choosing to decline some social invitations. I decided to focus on meeting my 'live line' as I call it which is the first manuscript deadline to wand to your editors and after that a re-draft and typeset.
- I reduced alcohol and caffeine consumption and increased drinking water, herbal teas and include additional vitamins and minerals in my vegetarian diet

For my second book, Mothers and Daughters I followed a similar process

- I diarised out full days of either six, nine or twelve hours writing and took short breaks to walk, dance, eat or snooze for 20 minutes to re-energise
- In addition to the above, I followed the same process as writing Find YOU, Find LOVE
- I wanted to add a vital research piece to this book. Before writing I read and digested information for three months by way of reading other books on the same theme, exploring psychology books based on Mother and Daughter relationships, I watched DVDs of films with Mothers and Daughters in conflict. I listened to songs in the same theme. I immersed myself in the subject to learn from a range of Mother and Daughter scenarios as well as working with case studies for the book
- I set up a series of case studies and sent out an online questionnaire to mothers and daughters across the globe who were interested in the research and to share their personal story in my book
- I had to work through the grieving process of mourning and my Mums death during this time, and she passed away part way through writing and was able to, with experience write about coming to terms with your relationship with your mother, 'even if she's gone.'

- I simplified my life and went without treats and social outings to fund the publication. I knew I had to share this book to help others and made a choice not to spend out on 'frivolous, unimportant things

For my third book Write from Your Heart my writing process was very different

- I followed many of the same principles as in books one and two
- I wrote parts of the book testing content with private journaling group of one hundred people as I went along.
- I took three months extensive research to include the history of journaling, diary-keeping, writing memoirs, reading books about writing and the science-based benefits gained from writing by hand including the benefits in mental, physical and emotional health.
- I've had to learn the technical side and how to set up a private social media group to trial new processes and test the material included in Write from Your Heart.
- I wanted to gain insights into the working group writing experience and delivery methods from those who were collectively journaling as I created the new material.

- I extended myself by exploring writing concepts and creating journaling exercises, materials and processes which were based on my own experiences and learning rather than showcasing other people's articles and ideas to a higher degree detailed in my first two books.
- I had to get out of my comfort zone to create and share my material from my heart. I learnt to recognise I have valuable experience to offer and not 'hide behind someone else's light' training courses, techniques and methods even if it has felt safe to do so in the past.
- I'm continually learning new ways of working as an indie author (self-published author) Each time I write a book I come to it from a new angle depending on my end goal and what I want to achieve for the book and my reader group.
- It has been challenging to complete this book to reach my planned goal date for my final manuscript amid unprecedented times, with the Coronavirus (COVID- 19) epidemic. I have loved ones with the symptoms and pray they and everyone on the planet including mother earth become wiser, stronger and collectively communicate first from our hearts and then our minds

- As a result of writing this book and trialling the material, I have become aware of the need to offer tailored writing retreats and support programmes for aspiring authors. Having access to therapeutic support as well as writing guidance, provides an opportunity to go more in-depth on a personal level and aids for emotional catharsis, which is paramount when writing and completing your first book.
- Writing is an emotional journey and to engage in an in-person, or online on a writing retreat where you have my sole focus can add depth to your writing experience and your creation.

Your first book is generally a steppingstone to additional books and acts as a catalyst to offer value to your readers. Making time to invest in healing the hurt within will support you long term as an author to continue writing your book series.

✓ Are you ready to get started on your writing project beyond journaling?

✓ Do you want more clarity around defining your ideal reader?

✓ Need assistance with goal setting and making an action plan to write and publish your book?

✓ You're in the right place at the right time.

You can read what others are saying and find out the full benefits of working with me on my website.

You can choose from a standalone 'Define Your Ideal Reader Breakthrough Blueprint Consultation,' or a support programme to receive regular coaching as you write your book. VIP Days and writing retreats are also available.

Go to www.wendyfry.com to check out my support options. When you leave a review on Amazon for Write from Your Heart, do let me know on booking and I will be sure to include a bonus gift for you.

MOVING BEYOND JOURNALING TO TRANSFORM THE AUTHOR WITHIN

Every books creation begins with making a start, pick up your pen and start writing from your heart – your journal is waiting - Wendy Fry

The subject of how to write a book is too broad to cover in this book, and I have included three recommended books which I have personally read which helped me to get started on my writing journey.

Write an Evolutionary Self Help Book – The Definitive Guide for Spiritual Entrepreneurs, Sasha Allenby

Catalyst – Speaking, Writing and leading for Social Evolution, Sasha Allenby

How to Write a Book, Get it Published and Keep ALL the Profits, Richard McMunn

There are thousands of books on writing which you may like to explore further. Ideally, with the support of a writing coach, you can be guided as to what genre of writing is the best fit for you.

TAKING INSPIRED ACTION TO SHARE THE VOICE OF YOUR HEART

Don't let your words die inside you. You've worked hard all your life to make something of yourself. I'll show you how to turn your words into a self-published memoir, self-help book or how-to transformation series. Remember your words and your story matter - Wendy Fry

If your life was a title of a book, what will you call it?

What is the subtitle, strapline or specific process you will be using to guide your reader?

How would the hardships you have lived through and the coping methods gained make a compelling guide for your readers?

Who will benefit from learning the exact strategies you used to overcome those setbacks?

Writing a book supports you to share your life story. Readers want real-life stories. They want to gain a sense of hope from someone who has been there, done it and got the t-shirt. No one else is you, and this is your superpower.

If your story is relatable and your readers identify with the pain and pleasure points, you have lived through; your book can be a catalyst for positive lasting change. Your readers have been searching for your book, don't disappoint them.

What is it about the title which hooks your reader?

Why is your message the exact call to action your readers want to hear?

How will your life experience change the life of your reader once shared?

Honour the life you have lived and the life of your reader by writing your story.

Whether in the form of a memoir, self-help guide, mind, body & spirit companion book or a fiction novel changing your story to create a different outcome, writing you will find nourishes your soul and heals your mind and the mind of your readers.

Your life experiences, your wisdom and the principles that supported you along the way need to be shared. When you write from your heart, those reading will be right there with you cheering you along and will be inspired to make profound shifts in their life when they relate personally to your story.

How will voicing your words, your despair, your breakthroughs and your successes guide your reader to turn the page in your book and their lives and begin their own life story differently?

Make contact to find out how to write from your heart support writing retreats and support programmes will help you complete your book. www.wendyfry.com

IT'S NEVER THE END – THIS IS JUST THE BEGINNING

Go deeper. Past thought into silence. Past silence into stillness. Past Stillness into heart. Let love consume all that is left of you - Kabir

Just for fun, you may like to also complete your biography or *'About Me'* section in your journal, adding whatever additional facts about yourself you would like others to know.

Favourite Quote: *Wherever you go - Go with all your heart – Confucius*

Favourite Film: The Wizard of Oz

Favourite Colour: Cerise Pink, closely followed by purple, turquoise, orange and green (The photographer who took my biography photo told me I looked like a fruit salad with a variety of colours I was wearing)

Favourite Pastime apart from reading and writing: Walking in Nature closely followed by dancing at any given opportunity

Favourite books: Seagull – Richard Bach, The Lion, The Witch and The Wardrobe C.S. Lewis and James and the Giant Peach Roald Dahl, The Precious Present – Spencer Johnson

Most loved possession: Wooden Buddha carving

Favourite Flower: Gerbera (because they always look happy)

Best Loved Music Track: Feeling Good – Nina Simone

Favourite Drink: Prosecco or peppermint tea (not together) not forgetting sparkling water

Favourite snack: Cheese and crackers with grapes on the side, yum!

Chocolate preferences: Mint Matchmakers, Mint Aero and anything posh

What I do poorly but still like to do: Sing

Greatest Love: Life, oh AND Cherry Garcia Ice cream

Life Mission: To continue to write and speak from my heart encouraging others to do the same

NOTES FROM THE AUTHOR

I write from my heart; I always have done. My aim with everything I write is to leave a positive legacy behind in the hope of those who read my words will hear their calling and live their life 'on purpose.'

I value life. I never used to. There was a time when I thought of ending my days. I'd had enough of it all. Have you been there too?

Sometimes when we find ourselves experiencing what feels like 'the dark night of the soul', it is in this place we see the light, when we find ourselves hopeless and on the brink of despair that is where we may hear our calling.

Use your past to work for you - don't run from it. You have work to do – the work of your heart.

Thank you for accepting the call.

When nothing is certain – writing is possible – Wendy Fry

CONCLUSION

You have the potential to become an author - Wendy Fry

To aspiring authors everywhere, I acknowledge your commitment to share the words of your heart to help others heal, transform and grow. Please know not only will your book reach those who need it most, energetically you are putting so much good out into the world. Your words are the legacy you leave behind.

'Words connect us. The gift of your words of wisdom may well save someone's life - Wendy Fry

APPENDIX

WRITING COACHING AND MENTORING SERVICES

When you're ready to go deeper into your writers' journey and work with me as your writing coach & mentor or as a ghostwriter Please check the criteria below and make contact.

Reach out if you feel we are a great fit and reach me at www.wendyfry.com

- ✓ **You are a heart-centred entrepreneur**
- ✓ **You have a unique message to share**
- ✓ **You desire to help others succeed**
- ✓ **You are a creative change maker**
- ✓ **You have great ideas and end goals**
- ✓ **You are a positive *'what's possible'* thinker**
- ✓ **You want to raise your game**
- ✓ **You are committed to making time to work in partnership with me**
- ✓ **You have the funds to get started on your project**
- ✓ **You can commit fully to writing in your own time**
- ✓ **If you require a ghostwriter, you have information to share with me in the form of ideas, existing books, blogs, articles, video's**

or talks so that I have a feel for you and the message you wish to share

- ✓ **You wish to source the details of my publisher who will guide you through the self-publishing process**

I look forward to supporting you on your author's journey to Write from Your Heart!

www.wendyfry.com

ACKNOWLEDGEMENTS

I wish to acknowledge you, the reader. Without you, this book would remain unread an amass of words floating in the ether.

It is my pleasure to connect with you through time and space. As we come to the end of this adventure, I invite you to begin a new one. From this day forth, write from your heart and allow your authentic voice to be discovered, supported and heard.

I know there is a book inside you. Perhaps there are several? I intend to inspire you to share your message, your passion and your purpose through the written word.

This book would not have been possible without my clients, workshop participants and willing case studies who trusted me enough to be vulnerable in sharing their written work. Thank you for your trust in me.

With loving thanks to my Mother Jeanette and Father Paul, who gave me the gift of life and my brother Colin who taught me how to shape some funky dance moves. My wonderful Nephew Harry, who calls me 'His Crazy Aunt.' It's true, I'm crazy about this young man, and he fills my heart with joy and love.

Massive hugs to my amazing friends especially 'THE HOGS' (Girlfriends with Hearts of Gold) Gill Shaw, Ann Whittaker, Deborah Marshall, Joanna Emmerson, Maaike Vlamm, Lucy Moreton, Lisa Rackham and Caroline Maidment, you are the best!

Special thanks go to Olive Webb, who was like a second mum to me; Olive picked me up many times when I fell. She showed me how to love.

Heartfelt gratitude goes out to my exceptional mentors: Margaret Biggs, Helen Stanbridge, Jane Taylor, Clive Levy, Curly Martin, Lexie Bebbington, Anne Jirsch, Karl Dawson, Sasha Allenby, Monica Cafferky, Silvia Hartmann, Joshua Brown and finally though in no way least, Richard McMunn. Thank you all for influencing my life positively.

To all the people who have caused me pain and discomfort in my life, without the challenges and experiences I had with you, I may never have found the path leading me to do the work I love and writing from my heart – so I thank you.

DEDICATION

Loving thanks to my mother Jeanette Cowell who indirectly inspired me as to who I can become

My mother taught me how to read and write as much as I hated learning the alphabet at the time sitting amongst balls of scrunched up paper crying my eyes out as I could not get it right the first time or the next. I am grateful for the legacy she left behind. To write from the heart, like a bird on the wing, flying high is freeing. Soaring above the past, looking back on how far I've come. I am genuinely grateful for my journey. I invite you, dear reader, to reflect on your life and acknowledge the personal wins. Why? Because of you, your words and your story matter.

From my heart to yours with love.

X Wendy

HOW YOU CAN HELP

I welcome your support to share the legacy of my words from my heart. Thank you for sharing the love.

How would you prefer to help me?

- Leave an Amazon review
- Share this link to my website www.wendyfry.com
- Share this link to my Amazon Author Page
- Gift copies of my book to reading and writing groups?
- Gift copies of my book to your friends, family and colleagues
- Random Acts of Kindness gifting copies of this book to a good cause, charity or leaving in a random place for someone unexpectedly to find

FREE RESOURCES & BONUS GIFTS

Thank you for reading. Write from Your Heart.

I love to give what I can make a difference in someone else's life. As a little thank you for staying with me on this voyage of personal discovery. I'm gifting you a FREE guided meditation to support you on your writing journey. Additional free resources are available at www.wendyfry.com

Send a direct email detailing your preferred choice of audio from the following options to info@wendyfry.com. Your audio will be sent to you by WeTransfer within a week of requesting.

Negative Memory Release

Are you fed up with reliving experiences from the past over and over? How often are you overwhelmed by your emotions or other people's? Whatever it is that's stopping you from living a joy-filled life and writing from your heart this guided meditation will support you in detaching from anger, anxiety, guilt, shame, and so much more. Begin today, leave your past in the past and continue your writing journey in a more positive, happy, confident and content frame of mind where you can share your authentic author voice with ease.

Anger Release

Learn the art of controlling your anger, low mood or depression with this guided meditation which will enable you to heal at the deepest level and share your truth succinctly. Anger is a healthy emotion if used wisely, and this guided meditation will help you to release unresolved anger enabling you to write from your heart. Anger hurts you more so than anyone else; it eats away at us and robs us of valuable time and energy. Listen to this audio to release past and current anger. Set yourself free today.

Saying Goodbye

Losing someone we love, whether through a relationship break up, or death is often one of the most challenging things we must go through. This guided meditation is ideal if you want to come to terms with a relationship ending or indeed finding a way to say goodbye to a loved one who has passed away. Allow yourself to grieve the emotions entirely and gain acceptance of what has come to pass. Your journal may act as a support guide where you can write your goodbye letter writing what you wish to express from your heart.

Emotional Calm

Worn out with being at the mercy of your emotions, sick and tired of feeling sick and tired? Ready to experience more fun and joy in your life and transfer that energy into your writing? This emotional calmness meditation will provide you with feeling freedom from your overwhelming emotions, allowing you to attain emotional calmness in any situation wherever you are. It will support you to enjoy the process of journaling and expressing who you are when you're at your best and help you to write and complete your first book aiding a sense of wellbeing when you listen in regularly.

Fear Release

When fear becomes destructive, it stops you from achieving the goals in life, which are essential to you. Whether it's a desire for happier relationships, improved health and emotional well-being or merely living a more abundant life, this guided meditation will support you in letting go of the past enabling you to create for yourself a happier future.

Forgiveness

We all at some time experience negative life events, situations and people, and we know we would not want to go through those experiences again. Often, part of us holds onto what happened as a form of self-protection. This guided meditation leads you to a place where you can draw a line under your past, supporting you to move forward to create a life free from the pain which resides within. Perhaps you will share your story of forgiveness in your journal.

Guilt Release

Guilt has a way of festering inside; it stops us living in the present and keeps us stuck in the past. Holding onto guilt not only hurts you, but it also prevents you from living a healthier and happier life. Use this guided meditation to let go of wherever it is you have been holding onto and end the pain and misery today. Making a mistake is part of life's learning, and by releasing guilt in your journal and with use of this audio, you are not only wiser you are free from the past which binds you.

Healing the Inner Child

Within you lies an 'Inner Child' with unmet needs, hopes and dreams. A child who may have experienced a lack of love, attention and affection, You and your inner child have been waiting for a long time to feel heard, supported, encouraged and loved unconditionally. This beautiful, guided meditation will help you in healing the hurt within, setting your inner child free to live life with a sense of fun and curiosity. Don't put off until tomorrow what you could do today; your inner child will be grateful to you. Use this meditation and your Journal to heal the hurts within.

Rebuilding Trust

What limiting beliefs do you have about yourself and others? Are you scared of being hurt, let, down, disappointed or rejected? You are not alone. If you've lost that loving feeling this guided meditation explicitly designed connect with that part of you who wants to love and be loved, that part of you who wants to trust again and is unsure where to start. This beautiful recording will guide you to a place of understanding and offer you hope for the future.

Back to the Womb

This delightful, guided meditation takes you back to experience a connection with your birth mother. Whatever your past or present circumstances with your mother this audio will guide you back home to you, the place where love resides, connecting you with a never-ending fountain of love within so you are truly free to write from your heart.

Self-Belief

Whatever your struggles, doubts or insecurities, this meditation leads you to experience feelings of calm, relaxation and inner peace wherever you are. When you connect with the stillness within, you can shut out all negative Influences from entering your life. Today is the first day of the rest of your life, and I know your future self will benefit from increased self-belief and writing from your heart?

To claim your free guided audio email Wendy at info@wendyfry.com stating the title of your chosen meditation. If you'd like to receive the full range of all eleven audios the bonus offer investment is £49. RRP is £110. Contact to request at info@wendyfry.com

AUDIO LISTENING AGREEMENT

All audios are copyrighted, which means they should not be shared with any third party or copied in any way.

Wendy makes no medical or psychological claims regarding these meditations. If you are suffering from a medical or psychological condition, please seek professional help from your GP or physician.

As the listener, you are accepting full responsibility and accountability for any life changes that occur as a result of listening to these audio recordings. Do not operate machinery or drive while listening to these audios. Ideally, you will be seated or laying down in a relaxing setting.

USEFUL RESOURCES

The Energy of Anxiety - Ann Bowditch

Future Vision Your Working Life:10 Strategies to Help You Get Ahead - Anne Jirsch

Write an Evolutionary Self Help Book – The Definitive Guide for Spiritual Entrepreneurs, Sasha Allenby

Catalyst - Speaking, Writing and leading for Social Evolution, Sasha Allenby

How to Write a Book, Get it Published and Keep ALL the Profits, Richard McMunn

Anne Jirsch – Future Life Progression Training www.annejirsch.com

The Energy of Anxiety www.energyofanxiety.com

BOOKS BY WENDY FRY

Find YOU, Find LOVE available on Amazon in e-book and paperback format.

Mothers & Daughters available on Amazon in e-book and paperback format.

CONTACT

Based in the United Kingdom Wendy works in person and online running retreats and workshops worldwide offering guidance as a writing coach, mentor and ghostwriter.

Tailored support programmes, workshops and writing retreats are available wherever you are in the world. Find out more at www.wendyfry.com

Contact the author directly for signed copies of her books with a personal message to inspire you at info@wendyfry.com

ABOUT THE AUTHOR

"I believe in being real. My wrinkles and scars, including the ones you can't see, make me whole. Don't let your fears define you; let them shape who you become." Wendy Fry

A book contains much more than words. An author's heart and soul are in there too - Wendy Fry

Having the title, *'author'* doesn't mean I'm a guru who needs to be bowed down to or held in revere. There is no need to stutter in my presence, put on your best voice or talk about the weather.

I too am a living, walking, talking breathing person with feelings, doubts and insecurities mapped on my face for good measure. Life has thrown me its fair share of curveballs and poop storms, enough to